Our Century

The Canadian Journey in the Twentieth Century

Robert Bothwell
and J.L. Granatstein

McArthur & Company

Toronto

First published by McArthur & Company, 2000
This paperback edition published by McArthur & Company, 2001
322 King Street West, Suite 402, Toronto ON M5V 1J2

National Library of Canada Cataloguing in Publication Data

Bothwell, Robert, 1944-
    Our century: the Canadian journey

Includes index
ISBN 1-55278-161-5 (bound)   ISBN 1-55278-251-4 (pbk)

1. Canada – History – 20th century I. Granatstein, J.L., 1939-   . II. Title.

FC600.B683 2000   971'.06   C00-931335-4

Composition and Design by *Michael P. Callaghan*
Cover by *Rocco Baviera/4 Eyes Art + Design*
Typeset at *Moons of Jupiter, Inc.*
Printed in Canada by *Transcontinental Printing Inc.*

10 9 8 7 6 5 4 3 2 1

The publisher would like to acknowledge the financial support of the Government of Canada through the Book Publishing Industry Development Program (BPIDP) and the Canada Council for our publishing activities. The publisher further wishes to acknowledge the financial support of the Ontario Arts Council for our publishing program.

for Norman Hillmer
With affection and admiration

And in memory of
Anne Hillmer

CONTENTS

Sir John A. Macdonald

Marshall McLuhan

Raymond Massey

Lester Pearson

John Diefenbaker

Illustrations by David Annesley, by permission of *Exile Editions*

Prologue

Almost one hundred years ago Prime Minister Sir Wilfrid Laurier commented that the twentieth century would belong to Canada. Though few Canadians today accept that claim, most think that Canada was, is, and will remain God's country, the golden land, the single best place in the world to live. It is pleasant, but scarcely important, that the United Nations and the World Bank share this view. What does matter is that Canadians believe it. Every poll confirms this assessment, including polls in Quebec.

Despite the challenges created by a difficult climate, Canada provides a democratic environment for a multiplicity of peoples to thrive in peace and freedom. It is a genuine land of opportunity too. When Jean Chrétien was a minister in the Trudeau government, he told his deputy minister, Tommy Shoyama, "You know, this has to be the most wonderful country. Here I am, a little guy from a working-class home who speaks fractured English and I can become finance minister ... And here you are, a Japanese Canadian accused of disloyalty in the war, and you can become deputy minister of finance. Where else in the world could something like this happen?" Almost nowhere, to be sure.

Moreover, Canada has played a wholly creditable role in the world in this century. It has broken its ties with Britain peacefully and become the multilateral nation-state par excellence. It has all the benefits of North America, with few of the drawbacks (the wars, assassinations, and racial strife) that make the United States such a complex and troubling neighbour. Without stretching words too much, the case can be made that Laurier was right.

Let us remember what Sir Wilfrid said and why he said it. "As the nineteenth century was that of the United States, so I think the twentieth century shall be filled by Canada," he told the Ottawa Canadian Club in 1904. Later that year he repeated himself, telling another audience: "I think we can claim that it is Canada that shall fill the twentieth century ... For the next seventy-five years, nay the next hundred years, Canada shall be the star towards which all men who love progress and freedom shall come." Why this reiteration of a theme? Laurier was in an election campaign, running for a third term at a time when the racial antagonisms between French and English which had been aggravated by the South African War a few years before were beginning to fade. The francophone Laurier was preaching racial harmony, holding out the promise of a great future for all Canadians. There were major issues that divided Canadians, but the prime minister genuinely believed that the development of the nation's wealth could unite everyone with confidence in the future. In his campaign and in his mind, the twentieth century really was Canada's. And, of course, Laurier won his election.

Today, not even Laurier could argue that Canada comes close to the United States in wealth or in military or economic power. By comparison, Canada is a success in a minor key. But if the case cannot be made that Canada dominated the twentieth century, we can and should believe that we had the best of it. Canada was and is a healthier society than its great neighbour.

The primary reason is the general quality of civility and decency that prevails in Canada. It is a joke that Canadians say "excuse me" more than they say "eh" and that they wait for the green light even when no cars are in sight. We really are earnest, well meaning, polite to a fault. But those are all virtues, even if Canadians sometimes forget this fact. Canada's cities, by comparison with those in the United States or in most of Europe, not only work but are safe and clean. The social safety net, though torn by deficit fighters in government and business, remains a moderately effective equalizer; medicare still functions, though not as well as five years ago; and, however severe they are, the disparities in income are less threatening to the body politic than in the United States. Canada also has its political buffoons, but deals with them in ways that usually do not turn into a media circus or paralyze the operations of government. Many critics argue that the heavy-handed ways welfare and health care "reform" were tackled in several provinces is an indication that Canadian civility is on the decline, and they may well be right. Still, even if they drew their inspiration from south of the border, in no province is the public and private discourse nearly as vicious as in the United States. Just watch the political talk shows on CNN for an evening to gauge the American mentality.

Even the 1995 Quebec referendum was an exercise in civility. The campaign, like the 1998 Quebec provincial election, was fought with enormous passion and was no model of democracy in action. There were inexcusable errors in voter registration, calculated lineups at the polls to wear down elderly No voters, and largely successful efforts to declare No ballots spoiled. But when the *Oui* and *Non* crowds came out of their respective arenas at the same time on October 30, 1995, after a night of tears and cheers, there were only a few shoving matches. Could any such event have transpired anywhere else in the world with so little violence? The calm in Quebec was so ... Canadian.

Americans might suggest that the referendum campaign showed that Canadians care little for their nation. Perhaps, but the spontaneous and huge rally in Montreal on the Friday before the vote should give the lie to that. Moreover, public calm reflects the tolerance and patience of Canadians, their sense that political disputes and even the possible dissolution of the nation can be discussed in a civil manner, however draining separatism might be and however much it debilitates the public will and slows investment. After all, Canadians have been peacekeepers around the world for almost a half-century. Our soldiers, French- and English-speaking alike, have seen Israel and its neighbours at war, Cyprus divided, Rwanda a genocidal bloodbath, and Bosnia and Kosovo in the throes of ethnic cleansing. There is the sense among those who have served on peacekeeping operations that what they have seen must never become a reality in Canada. "Nothing made me feel prouder of this country than serving abroad and seeing how others have it," a Québécois in the army told the media.

In other words, the military, the ultimate guarantor of the state, is determined that even a contested secession of Quebec will not turn to violence. With the example of their own Civil War before them, Americans may find this a peculiarly namby-pamby approach. Did Abraham Lincoln die in vain? But Canadians are not a messianic people; manifest destiny is not in the Canadian lexicon; and there is little desire to preserve Confederation against all odds. In effect, Canadians have decided that civility is more important than civil war, that separation is preferable to bloodshed. Who, looking at global slaughters, could disagree?

There is certain proof of this civility in the Canadian talent for absorbing a vast array of people. Capital-M Multiculturalism as a political policy remains contentious, but small-m ordinary citizen multiculturalism has been an extraordinarily positive force in Canada. It has leavened the solemnity of Anglo-Canadians with European *weltschmerz* and Chinese energy, and replaced glutinous Yorkshire pudding with dim sum and osso buco, pad thai and perogies. Toronto, the most racially mixed metropolis on earth, is now a great restaurant city with the best Chinese food outside Hong Kong — and, perhaps, Vancouver — on a good day! The Canadian ethnic mix — one in six Canadian citizens is an immigrant, compared with one in fourteen Americans — is a national strength. And Canadians in all their variety live together in decency and peace. Yes, there are hotheads, bigots, and tensions; yes, there has been rioting in Toronto, Vancouver, and Montreal. But compare our big cities to cities elsewhere, and they seem like pastoral oases. Why? Civility. Canadians, even those who have just arrived here, somehow breathe decency in the air. Words are the weapons, not guns, and in Canada the state offers a share of power and the ability to effect change to all. Civility lets us live and thrive.

This book is a history of Canada in Laurier's century, Canada's century, our century. It is a story of many successes and some failures. It is a tale of growth, development, and prosperity, and a history of inequality, injustice, and poverty. It is the story of a people who struggled to build a nation, succeeded sometimes and failed often, then continued to struggle forward.

Much has gone wrong at home, much blood has been spilled on foreign fields. But much has gone right, too, and Canadians need to recognize the success they have made of their country. This book is not puffery, not a text that omits the disasters. Overwhelmingly, however, it is a record of success because, happily, that is the way Canada's history in the twentieth century unfolded.

CHAPTER ONE

CANADA IN 1900

National Archives of Canada C6761, PA206669, PA133676

*T*he twentieth century began in Canada with a burst of optimism. Most Canadians celebrated 1901, not 1900, as the first year of the new and glorious twentieth century. The *Manitoba Free Press*, Winnipeg's principal newspaper, published some inspiring verse under the title "A Twentieth-Century Toast":

Opposite: Turn-of-the-century Canada was not rich, but it had industries, vitality, and domesticity.

> Hail! New Born Cycle, Hail!
> A Royal Greetings Waits Thee Here!
> May Peace and Happiness Be Thine
> May All Your Years Be Filled with Cheer!

Not all citizens took their "cheer" literally, the *Free Press* added. "The closing of the year was marked in Winnipeg by religious observances coloured with a deep and thoughtful fervour and as the bells pealed forth their announcements of the birth of a new century many of the worshipers made conscientious resolutions to improve the new era as far as possible by the example of their daily lives." The nineteenth century had, after all, been an age of improvement — and in Canada improvement had a spiritual as well as a physical dimension.

It was hard not to be optimistic. Look at Winnipeg. Well within living memory Winnipeg had been a fur-trading outpost, hundreds of miles and several months, by trail and portage, away from the nearest newspaper or telegraph or railway. The 1870s, 1880s, and the first half of the 1890s had been years of feverish speculation, alternating with disappointment and depression. But by 1900 Winnipeg was booming: as the sixth largest city in Canada, it surpassed Halifax and was soon to overtake the capital, Ottawa. Prosperity, real or prospective, brought people to the Red River. Prosperity paid for electricity and telephones — not just in Winnipeg, but in every sizable town or city across the Dominion of Canada. And Winnipeg, like Canada, was linked to the world by railway and telegraph, and, through the Atlantic and Pacific ports, by steamship.

As the century turned, newspapers told stories of great events in Canada and across the whole British Empire, of which Canada was a proud and active part. It was an empire on which the sun never set, patriots boasted, where lands of pine and palm all gazed raptly at the heart — imperial London. In South Africa an imperial war was entering

National Archives of Canada C3477

Above: Canadian troops camp in Bloemfontein, capital of the Orange Free State, after its capture in 1900.

its second year, after an inspiring season of victories for Canadian and other imperial troops. In England, Canada's queen, Victoria, was spending Christmas at her estate at Osborne, on the Isle of Wight, taking a respite from knitting socks for her soldiers at war in the far-off Transvaal. She had quite a choice of recipients: they might be

Official art: an artist's conception of Canadian troops in the battle of Paardeburg in 1900. Paardeburg was a decisive victory for the empire forces.

Painting by R. Caton-Woodville, National Archives of Canada C22006

British, Australians, New Zealanders, or perhaps South Africans, all fighting so that the tip of Africa might be British.

Most Canadians had never known another monarch. Victoria had lived and reigned so long — since 1837 — that she eclipsed other rulers, just as Great Britain's power and prestige eclipsed that

Courtesy of J.L. Granatstein

of other countries. Even in the republican United States, the second half of the nineteenth century was known as the Victorian Age, after the diminutive grandchild of George III, the king who had lost America back in 1776.

The queen was perhaps not the perfect example of every aspect of the Victorian Age. She only grudgingly accepted electric light for her palaces, and she drew the line at flush toilets. In an age of democracy, she travelled only to visit her many royal relatives. In politics she was an unreconstructed Tory, frowning on most political innovations conceived after 1840. Yet she was undeniably popular, due, primarily, to her best-known quality: respectability. The breath of scandal blew around the queen, but never touched her, even though Canadian newspapers eagerly reported royal scandals, such as fanciful royal relatives conceived by Victoria's own

The Boer War marked an advance in uniforms: troops dressed in a less conspicuous khaki colour and the uniforms were designed to be more comfortable and more practical.

5

National Archives of Canada PA185347

Queen Victoria greets wounded soldiers.

father while he served as a general in Canada around 1800.

Monuments to the queen were everywhere. She squatted on Ottawa's Parliament Hill, next to the House of Commons. The capital of British Columbia proudly called itself Victoria. There was Victoriaville in Quebec, and there were Victoria counties in Ontario and New Brunswick. Parks, streets, schools, even coloured prints on the walls of ordinary households all evoked Great Britain's and Canada's queen. Her success as a cultural phenomenon far surpassed her limited imagination and achievements.

Queen Victoria did not have power in the usual sense — certainly not the kind of power her royal ancestors had once wielded. She presided over a democracy — indeed, over several democracies. Canada was one of them. In Canada, every male who was also a British subject and twenty-one years of age was entitled to vote. Queen Victoria was almost the only female with a definitely recognized political role, for women were denied the franchise in Canada and almost every other jurisdiction on earth.

Most Canadians in 1900 voted for Wilfrid Laurier and his Liberal Party. Laurier had been prime minister since 1896 and, in the eyes of many Canadians, he was an odd bird. Fortunately for Laurier's career, they did not know how odd: those who knew him best thought he lacked faith in God, while those who knew him less well thought he was having an affair with his law partner's wife. Elegant, an inspiring orator, and an accomplished manipulator of people and events, Laurier was well qualified for his job. He believed in a political system that rewarded his followers and ignored his opponents. Loyal Liberals filled the ranks of road-menders and lighthouse-keepers from the Atlantic to the Pacific. The prime minister kept a close eye on government contracts — on the location of post offices or the purchase of boots for Canadian troops in South Africa. He needed an eye for detail: it reinforced his mastery of his cabinet and his party, and helped compensate for what many considered to be a defect — his Frenchness. Laurier was a French Canadian, a member of a minority language group at a time when government and patriotism both spoke English. Laurier, it was true, spoke English to perfection: he had learned it as a child and used it to graduate at the head of his class from McGill University. But language facility was not necessarily an advantage in Canada, socially or politically. "Learn English," a French-Catholic bishop told his parishioners, bowing to economic reality, "but learn it badly," thereby preserving their isolation and, with it, their language and faith. Laurier, so fluent and supple in both languages, set a poor example as far as many Catholic clergy in Quebec were concerned.

National Archives of Canada C147376

This Liberal election poster shows Laurier being cheered on by a youthful and athletic Canadian.

Equally deplorable to Laurier's many English-language detractors was another undeniable fact: the prime minister was a Roman Catholic. Protestants were still a majority in every province except Quebec. Canadians, Protestants or Catholics, took their religion seriously — and almost all Canadians were Protestants or Catholics. Jews, at 1.03 percent of the population, were the largest non-Christian group. In Quebec and Ontario, schools and other social agencies were organized on religious lines, though in Ontario the Protestant schools were officially "public" and theoretically non-sectarian.

Canada's Protestants and Catholics seldom came overtly to blows, but they continued the grievances and prejudices of their ancestors and kept a wary eye on those people who, like Laurier, bridged the gap between the sects. Religion and language (or, as people in 1900 thought of it, "race") were never far apart. Quebec was not only mainly French but also mostly Catholic. Fervent Catholics in Quebec denounced the "Laurier system" that sought cooperation with the hated English and the detestable Protestants; and fervent Protestants drew much the same conclusion, if from a different point of departure. In the election of 1900 a widely read Ontario newspaper, the *Toronto News*, urged its readers to vote against Laurier and the Liberals, "who have been stirring up race feeling in Quebec as a preliminary to restoring Canada to French dominion or building up an independent French state." A Laurier-hating priest in Quebec, Lionel Groulx, later penned a novel entitled *L'appel de la race* ["The Call of the Race"], whose main character abandons his Catholic but English-speaking wife and most of his family, corrupted by the English, in favour of the purity of blood, language, and religion. Canada, Laurier often reflected, was a very difficult country to govern.

If language and religion were divisive forces in Canada, politics, or at any rate political parties, were a unifying factor. By 1900 Canada's parties were about sixty years old — like Queen Victoria, they had been around as long as people could remember. To achieve power and hold it, a political party had, simultaneously, to express and transcend the status quo. It had to attract support across Canada's divisions by muting contradictions; to reward old followers without alienating new ones; and, above all, to bridge the gaps among Canada's regions. Canadian political parties had another characteristic: like those elsewhere, they were highly centralized and hierarchical, with great prestige and power vested in the party leader. Sir Wilfrid Laurier, an unusually successful politician, was leader of the Liberal Party for thirty-two years, 1887 to 1919. His most successful rival, Sir Robert Borden, led the Conservative Party for twenty — 1900 to 1920. Only death in one case, and voluntary resignation in the other, removed them from office, and their examples were mimicked across the country. The centralized party system contradicted not only Canada's polarized languages but also Canada's abundant regionalism.

If it was not race or religion, it was region. Canada was a huge country, three thousand miles across from sea to sea, and extending from the Great Lakes to the North Pole. Not all of it had yet been explored: several large uninhabited islands in the Arctic Archipelago remained to be discovered. The highlight of Canada's northern territories was the Yukon, newly organized around a gold rush in 1898. The Yukon temporarily boomed, but, like other gold rushes elsewhere, the boom was followed by a bust. The Midnight Sun of the North flamed, beckoned, and by 1901 sputtered. The Yukon and the rest of the North remained a piece of exotica, a lo-

National Library of Canada, Music Division

A Canadian version of the two-step dance craze, with a suitably Arctic motif.

cation for North West Mounted Police novels and the occasional thrilling motion picture. It also remained a dependency, a figment of another place's imagination, and an extension of southern society. When Canadians talked about "region" they did not mean the North (remote, barren, and, but for gold, as yet unprofitable).

In 1900 Canada was divided into four main regions and seven provinces. There were the three Maritime provinces — Nova Scotia, New Brunswick, and Prince Edward Island. (Newfoundland, proudly isolated, was an autonomous British colony, with its own distinctive political system.) These provinces were not unimportant, but they were small and remote geographically, isolated from the main population and industrial centres of the rest of Canada and North America. The national government used legislation and subsidies to promote industry in the Maritimes, especially in the coal-mining parts of Nova Scotia, and managed to produce a coal and steel complex centring on Sydney. Halifax, the capital of Nova

Scotia, remained a large port and manufacturing centre, though handicapped by distance from its markets. It was also a naval base, not for any local fleet, but for the North American squadron of the Royal Navy. Other Nova Scotians called Halifax "the garrison," and perhaps more than other Canadian cities it looked to its past rather than its present. In a sign of the times, the Bank of Nova Scotia abandoned its Halifax headquarters and moved to Toronto. Well-educated and ambitious, Maritimers gave a distinctive east-coast flavour to the Canadian school system. In general, however, the most important product of the Maritimes was people, who left in droves to populate the Canadian West.

Quebec, the next region over, was itself divided by language and location. There was a sizable English-speaking minority situated mostly around Montreal, and with rural branches to the east, west, and south along the American border. Quebec City, the provincial capital, had its own Irish and Catholic minority in the suburb of Sillery, but it was in Montreal where the *Anglais* were truly notice-able. Montreal was Canada's industrial, transportation, and finan-cial centre. Canada's largest and oldest bank, the Bank of Montreal, and its biggest railway, the Canadian Pacific, were headquartered in Montreal, along with most of their rivals. The homes of the man-agers of these companies spread north from the St. Lawrence up the slopes of Mount Royal — itself Canada's most beautiful urban park, designed by the American F.L. Olmsted. The "Square Mile" of mansions along Dorchester and Sherbrooke Streets, named after British governors, were remarkable for their size and luxury, accu-rately expressing the self-confidence and pride of their owners — Sir William Van Horne and Lord Shaughnessy of the Canadian Pacific Railway, Sir Herbert Holt, the utilities magnate, or Lord Atholstan of the *Montreal Star*. Stephen Leacock, a satirist of the period who was also a professor at McGill University, sketched out the "little toddling princess in a rabbit suit" who, with other privi-leged infants, might own half the city.

The English élite did not pretend to govern Quebec. That priv-ilege was reserved for a French-speaking élite, many from old fam-ilies. Only a few French-speakers populated the ranks of Quebec's millionaires, though there were some, including the Massons and the Forgets; instead, they dominated politics and related professions and, of course, the Catholic clergy. The post of provincial treasurer (finance minister) was always reserved for an English-speaker, and remained so down to the 1940s. As long as the Montreal English (or, rather, the Montreal English élite) remained dominant economically, across Canada as well as locally, they performed their function in Quebec. As for the future, any deviation from the established pattern was surely inconceivable.

Traditional Quebec houses showing characteristic sloping roofs, photographed in 1904.

National Archives of Canada PA206666

Yet the seeds of something different were present. Ontario, the next province to the west, was smaller than Quebec in physical size but larger in terms of population — as it had been since about 1850.

Ontario had a much larger and more fertile arable region than Quebec, a fact that translated into more farms, more farmers, and higher agricultural income. Toronto, the provincial capital and Ontario's

Toronto's busy Yonge Street in 1904. Note the absence of motorcars.

National Archives of Canada PA206667

largest city, was considerably smaller than Montreal, and lagged behind its Quebec rival in public monuments and private homes. Nevertheless, Toronto was a centre of light industry, and a wholesale and distribution centre for southern Ontario. It had its own financial sector, smaller than Montreal's, but still significant. Hamilton, to the west of Toronto at the head of Lake Ontario, was home to a burgeoning steel industry, with coal and iron ore — and capitalists, too — imported from the neighbouring United States. Like Cape Breton's, Ontario's steel industry was initially the outcome, in part, of government subsidies — tax relief from municipalities and tariff protection from Ottawa.

At the eastern end of the province was Ottawa, capital of the Dominion of Canada. When Queen Victoria first chose it as a colonial capital back in the 1850s, it was called "a Sub-Arctic lumber village." It was a village no longer, but home to platoons of politicians and accompanying civil servants. The climate remained sub-Arctic, and lumber, next to politics, was king: a large pulp and paper factory sat opposite the Parliament Buildings, across the Ottawa River in Hull, Quebec. The log booms on the river and the piles of wood chips may have reminded the politicians that Canada was a land of primary products, a developing country on the frontier of the world economy.

The politics of Ontario were a mixture of farming and development. Farmer voters looked after their own interests, and rural concerns dominated many of the issues of public life, from roads and markets to the prohibition of alcohol. Ontario politicians pursued the provincial interest as best they could, battling Ottawa for autonomy while demanding territorial expansion by carving up neighbouring territories; in 1912 Ottawa obliged, expanding Ontario (and Quebec and Manitoba) to the shores of Hudson Bay.

Manitoba, the next province, was the begin-

Summer vacations: women's tennis at the WaWa Hotel in northern Ontario.

National Archives of Canada PA195886

ning of the Prairie region. It was also the first provincial child of the new Dominion of Canada. Purchased from the Hudson's Bay Company by the Canadian government in 1869, the Red River Settlement (the area around the future Winnipeg) agreed to become Canadian only after an armed rebellion under the leadership of a charismatic local politician, the young Louis Riel. He, like many of the inhabitants, was of mixed French and Indian ancestry — the Métis. The rebellion was settled both by negotiation and by force: the negotiation produced guarantees of sorts for the property and lands of the Red River settlers as well as provincial status as the Province of Manitoba. Just in case, Ottawa sent an army made up almost entirely of British regulars to occupy the settlement. Riel fled, and many of his followers migrated further west, where in 1885 they would raise another rebellion. It, too, was similarly suppressed.

The acquisition of the Hudson Bay lands opened the Prairies to Canadian settlement, and settlement there was. The dominion government retained control of most of the land, though six million acres remained the private property of the Hudson's Bay Company. It then parcelled out the land to settlers, many of whom came from Ontario

Settlers seeking land: a "land rush" in Moose Jaw, Saskatchewan, 1909.

National Archives of Canada C5127

to Manitoba in the 1880s and 1890s. By contrast, settlers from Quebec were few and far between, though they survived through the twentieth century on the Canadian Prairies. The Ontario settlers transformed society in Manitoba, which in many respects became a miniature replica of the older province. Originally a bilingual province, with official standing for French, Manitoba was redefined in the 1890s as an English-language bastion, with only minor exceptions for French and other languages. The dominant language of the Prairies became, and remained, English.

There were, of course, other languages on the Prairies, as elsewhere in Canada. The First Nations — Cree, Assiniboine, Blackfoot, and many others — had lived on the plains for thousands of years. Nomadic hunters, they depended above all on the buffalo, which in earlier times roamed the grasslands in the millions. But by the time Canada acquired the plains and sent mounted police west in the 1870s, the buffalo were almost gone. European diseases had reduced their hunters to shadows of their former numbers and power. Canadian negotiators signed treaties with the Indian inhabitants of the Prairies: the Indians conceded land in exchange for a subsidized and protected status on reserves. In the minds of the Canadian government and its employees, it went without saying that the Indians, if they survived at all, would have to do so by transforming themselves into sober, religious, and educated replicas of the whites — at least as whites existed in their own imagination. To this end, the government encouraged Canada's various religious denominations to set up schools on or off the reserves, and set about modifying or even banning those native customs that seemed to be at variance with the customs of mainstream Canadian society. The effect was difficult to measure, as it was usually concealed in official reports by the government's local representatives, the Indian agents. What was absolutely certain was that indigenous numbers continued to decline: by the census of 1901, Indians represented barely more than 1.4 percent of the Canadian population. More remarkably, even on the Prairies they were, by the best available count, only a small minority of a population that had yet to see its greatest expansion.

The Prairies were governed from Ottawa as a kind of internal colony, the North-West Territories. Dominion civil servants administered lands and minerals directly, and a lieutenant governor ran everything else from the territorial capital of Regina. The North West Mounted Police had been raised as a special force in 1874 and sent west from Ontario: in their bright red tunics, the NWMP became a symbol of the West, of Canada, and of British order and justice, which

Canadians believed distinguished them from neighbouring disorderly Americans. Like many Canadian impressions of the United States, this one was exaggerated. Still, it proved enduring.

Colonists from Canada imported their politics as part of their culture. The two main Canadian political parties, Liberals and Conservatives, soon established branches in Manitoba and points west. Liberals and Conservatives gave leadership to a growing demand in the Territories for provincial status and greater autonomy. For a time the need for a united autonomy movement submerged ordinary partisan considerations, but everyone knew that once that demand was satisfied, the hereditary politics of eastern Canada would emerge in the West too.

British Columbia was different in this respect, as in many others. If the Prairies were looking up in 1900, British Columbia had its doubts about the future. Certainly it had little to boast about in its recent past. Barely 350,000 people lived in the province at the beginning of the twentieth century, scattered along the coast and in interior

Traditional houses in a native settlement at Blunden Harbour, BC, c 1900.

National Archives of Canada PA194985

valleys, with only the railway to link them. The readiest source of immigrants for British Columbia was the Far East, specifically China and Japan, but the white majority in the Pacific province emphatically preferred to keep it British.

British Columbia was home to abundant minerals and forests. These resources attracted capitalists, and the capitalists hired workers. Mining and forestry were lucrative enough, but conditions and wages in those industries did not keep pace with the prosperity of other sectors of the economy. It is not surprising that miners in British Columbia, like those in Nova Scotia or the United States, supported radical trade unionism and radical politics. American unions and immigrant British socialists added spice to the brew. There was one other ingredient: BC workers were also racial exclusionists, seeing immigration from China and Japan as a means to drive down wages and break the trade union movement. Radical trade unionism was, however, only one side of a deeply polarized system of politics in British Columbia. The premier, Sir James Dunsmuir, was a mine owner and the province's largest employer. While he invoked patriotism and class interest to keep American unions at bay, he was ready to use force if necessary.

Dunsmuir was a Conservative, and some of his opponents, especially moderate trade unionists, were Liberals — or, at least, allies of the Liberals. The moderates were squeezed out by more radical opponents, however, with the result that British Columbia failed to develop a viable political centre. The alternatives in British Columbia, much more starkly than elsewhere in Canada, were Left and Right, a pattern that would persist throughout the twentieth century.

Fortunately, prosperity made governing Canada and its parts a little easier, and Canadians' ignorance of the outside world made the task easier still. Of all the countries in the outside world, only Great Britain and the United States had much reality for Canadians, partly because so many immigrants came from Great Britain and so many Canadians had left for the United States in the thirty years before 1900. Canadians accepted, though with some difficulty, that the United States was a much more prosperous country and that individual Americans were almost bound to be better off than their Canadian cousins. Great Britain, too, had a higher standard of living than Canada, but that was mitigated by the unequal distribution of income in the Old Country, which stimulated emigration to the colonies from less advantaged groups. Canadians did not generally know that their standard of living was lower than Australia's, and quite possibly beneath that of Argentina.

Below:
Parlour of
wealthy home,
Edmonton,
c 1902.

Provincial Archives of Alberta, E. Brown Collection, B 4678

Top right:
Pay day at
Northwest Bay
lumber camp,
Rainy Lake, 1899.

Right:
Boy worker,
c 1900.

How could this be? The visible progress and prosperity of the Canadian cities and the modern standard of living enjoyed by the citizens of Winnipeg suggested otherwise. But only a minority of Canadians lived in cities even by the generous standard used by the Canadian census, which counted any settlement of more than 1000 souls as "urban." Life on farms was, by and large, poorer and more primitive: no indoor plumbing, no electricity, and few services, except those of religion and the post office. To the gulf between English and French, between Protestant and Catholic, there

was added the gulf between city and country.

Moreover, Canada's wealth was commonly defined as Canada's primary products: what could be harvested from the soil, dug from the ground, or cut down from the land. Life in lumber camps or mining villages was tough, harder even than on the farms. It was the life of an employee rather than the life of an independent farmer, but the pay was more reliable, if low, and seasonal workers moved from farm to forest and back, as the harvest dictated. To jaundiced urban dwellers, it seemed that the main requirement for

the Canadian workforce was brawn rather than brain. Muscular strength and physical skill were what the economy needed, but the greatest rewards for toil were not often found in lumber camps and mining towns.

It was this realization that fed discontent in British Columbia, Nova Scotia, and at points in between. "Century to Begin with Big Strike: Fully 3000 Cape Breton Miners Will Leave Work Today," the *Free Press* informed its readers on January 1, 1901. In 1900 British Columbia fishermen went on strike, and, though their protest was broken by the intervention of the militia, they went out again in 1901. Trade unions were nothing new in Canada, nor were strikes. Not surprisingly, unions and strikes were most common in those sections of the economy that lagged behind the general prosperity, and mines and mining were one such area.

It may seem curious that radicalism did not spread to the cities. Within cities there were great social differences and economic disparities. Slums existed in every Canadian city of any size, and conditions in them alarmed the new and growing profession of social workers. The defining condition of an urban slum in 1900 was something that, in rural Canada, was an ordinary fact of life — an outdoor privy. Forty or fifty years before, outdoor privies had been practically universal, so, to older Canadians, it was a sign of progress that they were now considered a sign of poverty and deprivation. In Montreal, according to a prominent social critic and would-be reformer, fully half the homes in an area "below the hill" — beneath Mount Royal — had outdoor toilets. Sewers and sewage treatment plants, and municipal zoning to enforce better housing, became the goal of urban reformers in Canadian cities — the first tangible objective of the new century.

National Archives of Canada C30936

Reformers were not lacking in rural Canada, but unless they were connected to the organizations and money of the cities, their success was sporadic. Like the boom-and-bust crop cycle, rural reform was dominated by weather on the one hand and international markets on the other — both beyond control. Politics linked city and country, but in a highly structured and balanced way. Besides politics and government, there was only one other organizational link — religion. Organized religion had its own structures and politics, and they were sometimes closely linked to the other secular politics. At the end of the nineteenth century, much of the organized religion proved less self-confident and more permeable by new ideas than the secular political system. This openness was particularly true of the Methodists, the largest Protestant sect in Canada and the wealthiest.

Canadian families in 1900 were considerably larger than in 2000: in all but wealthy families, doubling-up children in bed was commonplace.

The Methodists, like other churches and virtually every other Canadian institution, were at the official level composed of men. Women comprised almost half the population, but they were completely unrepresented among the politicians, bankers, clergymen, and corporate magnates who made up Canada's various élites. Women were not entirely without rights, but the courts had yet to define them as "persons," and it was difficult, though not impossible, for women to live autonomous lives. Joining a nunnery was, among Catholics, one way out, though escape from male domination was not the only reason. Women needed an escort to go to the theatre or to a restaurant. Nor could women receive gentlemen callers, without grave damage to their reputation. The social constraints that Canadians applied to themselves caused visitors to exclaim on the narrowness and provincialism of Canadian society. "The manners of the Torontoese," a British immigrant exclaimed in 1894, "are delightful, [but] their customs are beastly."

There were, it was true, a few women who managed to advance themselves. The Ontario provincial government forced a reluctant University of Toronto to admit women in 1884, and by 1900 Canada boasted a very few women doctors and lawyers. Only nursing and teaching were respectable destinations for young women seeking employment before or instead of marriage. There were also opportunities in offices, though at the turn of the century they were small in number: the dominion government employed only seventy-two women in 1901. And only through inheritance could women expect to be or become wealthy in their own right.

Wealth sat easily on the shoulders of some Methodists, such as the Toronto department store owner Timothy Eaton and the meatpacker Sir Joseph Flavelle. They used their wealth for charity and supported the good works of urban missionaries. They certainly did not question a system that made their charity possible, and they would, at first, have been surprised and pained to discover that not all their co-religionists thought as they did. As of 1900, dissent was a small thing, imported from abroad, and imperfectly applied to conditions at home. Discontent was something that was surely susceptible to progress and prosperity. The nineteenth century had shown the way; now it was up to the twentieth to apply what the nineteenth had discovered. Given a solid patriotism and a stable world, there was no reason to believe that the new century would disappoint.

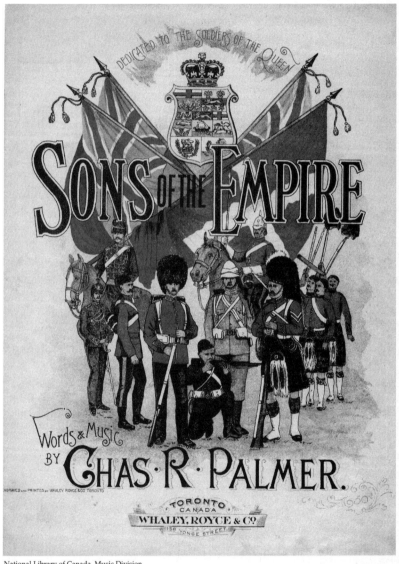

National Library of Canada, Music Division

Songwriters outdid themselves appealing to the patriotic fervour evoked by the South African War.

A NATION
OF IMMIGRANTS

*O*ne historian had it precisely right. "Canada is a peculiar nation," he wrote. "Peopled by immigrants, it is a country that hates immigrants." Its space unpopulated, its businesses desperate for customers, its politicians eager to prove that the twentieth century was certain to belong to Canada, the nation nonetheless looked askance at all those who tried to enter. Humorist Stephen Leacock was not joking when he wrote about immigration: How could we form a nation out of the "dirtiness of the Doukhobours" and the "hungriness of the Hungarians"? What, he wondered, could tie a country together that let in Southern and Eastern Europeans, Chinese and Japanese, Americans, blacks, and, yes, even the British? Had Canada become the dumping ground for the refuse of the world?

Opposite: Depending on where they settled, immigrants could benefit from hydro — and music — as Canadians did.

National Archives of Canada C681

Doukhobor women pulling a plough in western Canada. Such ways were alien to most Canadians.

Some of Leacock's contemporaries fretted in similar ways. Winnipeg Methodist preacher J.W. Sparling proclaimed: "There is a danger and it is national. Either we must educate and elevate the incoming multitudes or they will drag us and our children down to a lower level." The premier of Manitoba, Rodmond Roblin, was even bleaker in 1907. In five or ten years, "the foreign-born citizens of western Canada could if they chose take all matter of government absolutely into their own hands." The British race was in danger of being swamped. Sir George Foster, a federal Tory politician, agreed. The "quality of population counts much more than the quantity. Five thousand first-class immigrants," he said, "are much better than 50,000 of a class that it would take a generation or two to bring up to the right standard." And that standard, of course, was British Canadian.

A later writer, Mordecai Richler, had one of his characters in his novel *Solomon Gursky Was Here* expatiate on the Canadian condition. "Canada is not so much a country as a holding tank filled with the disgruntled progeny of defeated peoples. French Canadians consumed by self-pity; the descendants of Scots who fled the Duke of Cumberland; Irish the famine; and Jews the Black Hundreds." Then, he went on, "there are the peasants from the Ukraine, Poland, Italy and Greece, convenient to grow wheat and dig out the ore and swing the hammers and run the restaurants, but otherwise to be kept in their place." As for the others, those who had arrived a generation or two earlier and established a life in Canada: "We do our damn best to exclude more ill-bred newcomers, because they remind us of our own mean origins in the draper's shop in Inverness or the *shtetl* or the bog." Bleak as this view was, it had the ring of truth.

Why were Canadians so chary of letting newcomers in? In part, there was a sense that those who had been here from the earliest days of white settlement had earned the right to determine who else came in. At the turn of the century no one considered that the aboriginal peoples had any say in the matter. There was also a vaguely triumphant view that *la survivance* had proved successful in fostering the French race in Canada, while the United Empire Loyalists, those losers of the American Revolution, similarly had built a home in the wilderness. But above all there was fear that newcomers would dilute the attitudes and attack the positions that English and French Canadians had built up. And those attitudes had overtones of superiority: superiority to the Americans, who were a democratic rabble in contrast to the more ordered, monarchist Canadians; superiority to the British, who had not been toughened by the fierce extremes of weather, as Canadians had, and who had either been debauched by luxury or undermined by abject poverty; superiority to everyone who was not white and Christian, because those characteristics were by definition superior.

Yet Canadians had little to feel superior about. The nation had progressed since its origins, but nowhere as quickly as had been predicted. Immigration had been slow to develop. In the 1870s it averaged about 30,000 a year; in the 1880s, about 85,000; in the 1890s, for much of the decade a time of depression, no more than 40,000. British immigrants, who might have been expected to come to Canada to remain within the British Empire, did not. In the 1890s 1.1 million Britons emigrated to the United States, while only 187,000 came to Canada. Worse still, more people left Canada in most years — primarily to the United States — than arrived. In the last two decades of the nineteenth century, for example, 1,600,000 Canadians, most born in the dominion, emigrated to the States, while only 1,225,000 new immigrants came from overseas. This simple fact, this certainty that the sons and daughters of the native born, both English- and French-speaking, were fleeing Canada in search of opportunity, better land on the Great Plains, and more higher-paying jobs in the mill towns of New England guaranteed that those who remained had to believe themselves superior. How else could they explain why they stayed?

Those who did stay bitterly mistrusted each other. The British Canadians, by the turn of the century a clear majority in the Dominion of Canada, believed that the Québécois were simple, priest-ridden peasants who were doomed to inferiority, at least until they learned English and had the good sense to become Protestant. The French Canadians thought the *Anglais* were all but godless, money mad, and intent on dragging them into every British war. All that united French and English speakers was the certainty they were both better than everyone else. Immigrants were barely tolerated, treated abominably, and guaranteed at best a second-class status.

Even the English and Scots immigrants were scorned by the English-speaking. The lower-class English were scum, the good citizens of Toronto or Winnipeg or Vancouver claimed, the sweepings of the London or Liverpool streets. Their presence in Canada was "a mistake," one for which the government was blamed. Young boys and girls were taken from orphanages or from destitute families and shipped to Canada by various "welfare" schemes, to populate the colonies with British stock and rid Britain of a portion of

Photographer William Topley, National Archives of Canada PA010226

Scots immigrant family arriving in Canada in 1911. Many immigrants returned home, beaten down economically and appalled by the cold weather.

its urban poor. Sometimes young criminals, who a century before would have been transported to Australia, found themselves banished to Canada on one of these schemes. The Reverend J.S. Woodsworth, later the saintly founder of the Cooperative Commonwealth Federation, often told the story how a magistrate had chastised a young hoodlum: "You have broken your mother's heart, you have brought down your father's grey hairs in sorrow to the grave. You are a disgrace to your country. Why don't you go to Canada?" Woodsworth, like other social workers in the teeming tenements, worried that these wretched British men, women, and children could never overcome their origins to become free citizens in a democratic society. How on earth could they be Canadianized? The upper-class British migrants were equally suspect: they assumed that Canada was theirs for the taking, and the native-born despised them for their uppity airs and accents. The Irish Catholic immigrants were simply unspeakable in the eyes of all Canadians, especially the Protestant Ulster Irish, who kept the old feuds alive in Canada through the Loyal Orange Lodges.

Canadians were not, then, a tolerant lot at the turn of the century. The French speakers had come to Canada in the seventeenth century for the most part and, thanks to an extraordinary birth rate, had multiplied to be some 1.6 million by the beginning of the 1900s. Insular and inward-looking, the *Canadiens* resented the English speakers who owned the mines and factories and ran most of the larger businesses in Montreal and Quebec City. The *Anglais* were bad enough, but the new immigrants, and especially the Jews who poured in from the *shtetls* of Eastern Europe to escape the Czarist pogroms, were an abomination. Concentrated around Saint-Laurent and Main in Montreal, eating different foods flavoured with unusually pungent spices, wearing different clothes, and praying in strange tongues to a different God, the Jews seemed to threaten Quebec's sense of itself. Moreover, as the Bible noted and the *curés* repeated frequently, the Jews had killed Christ. Anti-Semitism became rife in Quebec, fostered by parish priests who warned of racial pollution.

Montreal was no different in its attitudes from Toronto or Winnipeg or anywhere else that Jews settled. In the Ward, the heart of downtown Toronto that became the immigrant quarter, living conditions were deplorable. Two or three families, with several broods of children, frequently occupied a small house — sometimes just a small flat — and the resulting sanitary conditions appalled good middle-class burghers who somehow assumed that, without money and only the most menial work, "these people" could live decently if they wanted to. The outcasts of Europe, the Jews were now living in filth in Toronto the Good. Over time, the Jewish tinker or peddler, beating a decrepit nag through the streets and calling for rags and bones, became a familiar sight. In the rural parts of Canada, Jewish hawkers sold everything imaginable from their wagons or backpacks — needles and thread, pots and pans, and other gimcrackery. This was useful work, most agreed, but once one Jew got in to Canada, he sent money back to Lodz or Minsk to bring in more of his family.

In Montreal the Jews began to take over the needle trades, sewing garments for men and women in factories that were little more than sweatshops or through grossly underpaid piecework farmed out to families working at home.

It was not that Canada actively sought out Jews as immigrants. Immigration policy was slapdash for most of Canada's history: anyone who turned up aboard ship in Halifax or Montreal and disembarked was an immigrant — unless he or she was a pauper, prostitute, or criminal, or proved to be illiterate, alcoholic, crippled, syphilitic, or mentally unstable. In effect, there was entry for all, and especially for the "preferred" classes, who were always British or American. Attempts to recruit the French from France failed dismally, so Quebecers never developed an attitude towards their transatlantic cousins. The highest barriers were erected for non-whites.

The Chinese — who most definitely were not wanted — had to pay a tax of $50 a head, a very large sum in 1900 dollars. In 1903 this tax was raised to $500, the equivalent of at least $20,000 today. Railway contractors had imported Chinese labour to help build the Canadian Pacific Railway through the Rocky Mountains, and many had died in the process. The survivors' efforts to bring over their families foundered on Canadians' endemic anti-Asian racism, which led to the escalating head tax. Those Chinese who could scrape up the money were allowed into Canada, over strong opposition from British Columbia's labourers and middle class. The Chinese, according to a royal commission that reported in 1902, were "a foreign substance within, but not of our body politic ... a continual menace to health ... obnoxious to a free community and dangerous to the state." There were anti-Chinese riots in Vancouver in 1887 and anti-Asian riots in 1907, and the local Asian community lived in fear. The city government and local residents saw them as unsanitary; they feared, because the Chinese were almost wholly a male society, that white women might fall prey to their opium, gambling, and sexual needs and end up as "white slaves." Chinatown, one preacher declared, was "wickedness unmentionable." The Vancouver health inspector observed In 1902: "The Japs try to obey the laws, but the Chinese are always on the lookout to evade them."

*I*mmigration—
provided it came
from Britain, northern
Europe, and the United
States—was welcomed
by most Canadians. But
immigrants from the
rest of the world were
ordinarily not wanted.
Indians, or East
Indians, as they were
usually called, were
as unwelcome as
Chinese or Japanese,
but because India was
part of the British

In May 1914, the *Komagata Maru* arrived at Vancouver with 376 prospective East Indian immigrants and spread racial fears among those whites who believed Indians incapable of assimilation into Canadian society. After a tense standoff, the HMCS *Rainbow* standing by, the vessel returned to the Far East with its passengers.

Vancouver Public Library 6228

Vancouver Public Library 6231

Not that the Japanese were any more desirable as immigrants in the eyes of British Columbians. Establishing a toehold in Vancouver, Steveston, and the Queen Charlotte Islands, the Japanese were even more feared than the Chinese, in part because Japan was beginning to be a world power. Japan's 1902 alliance with Great Britain constrained the government in any action to keep its people out of Canada. The Japanese were popularly denounced as "the yellow peril," and newspapers and both federal and provincial politicians demanded that British Columbia be kept a "white man's country." In 1907 a "gentlemen's agreement" between Tokyo and Ottawa limited immigration from Japan to 400 adult males each year.

Immigrants soon put down roots, adapting to Canadian ways. This Japanese Canadian hockey team played in Vancouver in 1919-20.

National Archives of Canada PA117267

Indian immigrants (usually called "East Indians" to distinguish them from aboriginal peoples) were equally unpopular. British subjects they may have been, but the Sikhs, Hindus, and Jains were regarded as unassimilable in a white man's society. A boatload of Indians that approached Vancouver's harbour in the spring of 1914 caused near panic in British Columbia and, after a two-month-long standoff, Canada's tiny navy — the already obsolete cruiser HMCS *Rainbow* — escorted the *Komagata Maru* back out to sea. Canada, as H.H. Stevens, the Conservative member of parliament for Vancouver, proclaimed, had "to keep pure and free from the taint of other peoples." "The immigrant from Northern Europe is highly desirable," he said on another occasion, "the immigrant from Southern Europe much less so, and the Asiatic ... is entirely undesirable."

Attitudes changed with the beginnings of an economic upturn and, after the accession of Wilfrid Laurier and the Liberal Party to power in 1896, massive immigration became a major government goal. John A. Macdonald's National Policy had been premised on the tariff, the railway to the Pacific, and the settling of the Prairies. The railway and the tariff were now in place; it was time to get immigrants.

It was long past time to do so. From 1870 to the late 1890s, people had trickled rather than flooded into the Canadian Prairies. On average, only 3000 farms a year had been established on government lands in a system known as "homesteading." Part of the reason was the attractiveness of the United States — a better climate, meaning a longer growing season, and often better land. By the 1890s, however, American free land for settlers was used up and, miraculously, just after the turn of the new century, a Canadian scientist developed an earlier ripening variety of wheat, called Marquis. The scientist, Charles Saunders, was knighted; his Marquis wheat went on to dominate crops across the plains. Now, surely, it would be Canada's turn.

In Clifford Sifton, his Manitoban minister of the interior, Laurier had the energetic mover and shaker he needed to ensure it was Canada's century. The Immigration Department had been a backwater of incompetents, paper pushers who failed to attract desirable settlers to the dominion. Now there were new men and new money for a massive advertising campaign in Britain, the United States, and Europe to trumpet the virtues of Canada. Under Sifton's lead, pamphlets with titles such as *The Wondrous West, The Last Best West,* and *The Land of Opportunity* were printed in huge quantities and many languages. By 1902 there were two million copies of twenty-three different pamphlets, and, four years later, 4.5 million copies. The prose radiated optimism: "The first foot of soil in Manitoba, Saskatchewan, and Alberta is worth more than all the mines from Alaska to Mexico," one said. Photographs pictured mature trees, rolling grasslands, and full summer, for Canadian winters were not considered an attraction. Journalists from far and wide were invited on tours to see what Canada had to offer.

More to the point, the Dominion Lands Act promised each new immigrant 160 acres of free land on fairly easy conditions. Immigrants were free to go wherever they chose in the West so long as the land had not already been set aside for farming, a timber lease, or an Indian reserve. This offer was irresistible, especially since the free land in the United States had all been allotted. For those with means, the Department of the Interior offered some useful information: land within 5 miles of the railway should sell for $10 an acre; an acre of wheat could be farmed for $7.50 and produce 20 bushels of grain at 68 cents a bushel; $1000 would buy a house and barn, livestock ($40 for a cow, $5 for a sheep), a wagon, and ploughs. And, for the adventurous young woman in search of a husband, there were 80,000 more men than women on the Prairies in 1906. Go West, young lady!

Sifton was convinced that his program would succeed. What Canada needed, he said, was farmers and farm labourers, men and women who could open up the Prairies. What Canada did not want were labouring men and mechanics, workers who would head for the cities and bring political radicalism and bad habits in their baggage. "Agriculture," Sifton asserted, "was the foundation of all real and enduring progress," not trade unionist troublemakers who would fill up the city slums. What he wanted, he said in a famous phrase, was "a stalwart peasant in a sheepskin coat, born on the soil, whose forefathers have been farmers for ten generations, with a stout wife and a half-dozen children ... We do not want mechanics from the Clyde — riotous, turbulent and with an insatiable appetite for whiskey. We do not want artisans from the southern towns of England who know absolutely nothing about farming."

The minister struck deals with shipping companies to scout out likely immigrants across Britain and Europe. His agents papered

Britain and Northern Europe as far east as Moscow with pamphlets extolling the virtues of Prairie farmland. Considering that Canada was competing with Argentina for good immigrants, Sifton felt that his deals with the immigrant companies were sound economics.

Sifton's agents also ventured into the United States, where there were tens of thousands of farm labourers who had arrived in the West too late to get free land in Oklahoma or North Dakota, but who might prefer the chance to own their own quarter-section in Saskatchewan or Alberta. Americans might not have been subjects of the queen, but, in Sifton's eyes, they were "of the finest quality and the most desirable settlers." And he was right, because Americans knew more than Europeans about North American conditions and methods.

The results of Sifton's campaign were astonishing, helped by improving economic conditions in Canada and deteriorating political conditions in much of Europe. People poured into the dominion in unprecedented waves. In 1900, 41,000 came; in 1903, 138,000; in 1906, 211,000; in 1910, 287,000, and in 1913, the immigration boom year of all time despite unemployment and economic slowdown, 400,870 immigrants arrived in Canada.

The change was dramatic. First, the Prairies began to fill with people. Cities like Edmonton, Saskatoon, Medicine Hat, and Lethbridge sprang into existence as functioning towns with a complete infrastructure. Calgary, for example, had a population of 4000 in 1901, but was a real city a decade later. The population of the three Prairie provinces was close to two million by 1921, a massive jump in two decades. At the same time, the country's Gross National Product doubled between 1900 and 1914, as did the production of wheat. New jobs were created, new factories opened their doors, new farms came into production. The first decade

of the century, in fact, produced the first net gain of immigration over emigration since Confederation — and by the huge margin of 810,000. The West was won.

Immigration definitively and decisively altered the composition of Canada. Although immigrants from Britain made up half of all who came, the new mixture was startling. In the 1901 Census, Canadians had listed their origins: British, 3 million; French, 1.6 million; other Europeans, 500,000; Asians, 23,000; and aboriginals, approximately 125,000. A decade later, there were 4 million of British origin, 2 million French, 1 million other European, 43,000 Asian, and some 105,000 aboriginals. Equally significant, the "other Europeans" tended to stay in Canada, while many American migrants returned home, and some of the British emigrated to the United States if they could or returned to the United Kingdom. The makings of multicultural Canada were in place.

Family events always drew crowds in their best clothes, as this Ukrainian wedding did in western Canada in 1911.

To the horror of many British-Canadian Protestants, large numbers of the newcomers were Roman Catholic, Ukrainian Orthodox, or Greek Orthodox. In 1901, 2.2 million of Canada's population of just over 5.3 million were Catholic; a decade later, Catholics numbered

National Archives of Canada PA088572

OUR CENTURY

2.8 million, and, in 1921, there were 3.4 million in a population of 8.8 million. Given the higher birth rate of the French-speaking and Roman Catholic segment of the population, it seemed only a matter of time before Canada would have a "Papist" majority. This projection troubled many of the English-speaking, especially the hardline Orangemen of Ulster Irish descent who believed that Canada, like Ireland, was slipping away. Religion had been the major fault line of Canadian politics for at least a generation, spawning the anti-Catholic Protestant Protective Association and the Equal Rights Association in the 1880s and 1890s, and now immigration was changing the battle lines — against Protestantism. This swing was yet another reason to oppose the flood of newcomers.

The immigrants all found it difficult to survive on the Prairies — no matter where they came from or whether they had paid their way across the Atlantic at $20 a head or accepted assistance from an emigration company or a charitable society. The towns were widely separated, and the Canadian Pacific Railway, which carried the immigrants westward in sparse Colonist Cars with rough benches, primitive sanitary facilities, and only a pot-bellied stove for heating and cooking, often pulled the spikes on the tracks and pushed the carriage into the unbroken Prairie to be collected later. "Your land," the immigrant might be told, "is twenty miles that way."

That land was prairie that had never seen a plough, land without much firewood, and sometimes without water other than the fetid contents of a slough. Or else it was the bush country of the northern parkland, often stony, sandy, or marshy. The first home was frequently a sod hut, shaped out of blocks of mud and grass. The first crop, planted by hand after the ground had been broken by a single-blade plough, grew from seed offered by the Crown, and the growing season was short. Until Saunders developed his quick-ripening Marquis wheat, it was a race each year to see if the crop could be harvested before winter came roaring in.

Immigrants often settled en bloc, forming a homogenous ethnic community. Ukrainians did so frequently out of choice, but also because government agents liked the idea, believing they would then require less public assistance. But the settlers already present on the Prairies reacted vehemently. The Nor'wester, a Manitoba news-

paper, argued in 1897 that such a system was "a positive misfortune for an enlightened community ... Both economically and socially they will lower the standard of citizenship ... Not only are they useless economically and repulsive socially, but they will constitute a serious political danger. They are ignorant, priest-ridden and purchasable." Corrupt politicians, the newspaper argued, could buy a few thousand votes and decide the future of Manitoba. The vehemence of the language, the certainty that the immigrants were ignorant peasants, were striking. Politicians argued that any decent Canadian, faced with such neighbours, would pull up stakes and leave for the United States. After all, native-born Canadians had moved west "because the British flag flies over it," the *Winnipeg Telegram* said in 1899, and because they wanted "to remain Britishers among British people." Instead, they were "hemmed in by a horde of people little better than savages — alien in race, language, and religion, whose customs are repellent and whose morals they abhor."

In such circumstances, it took courage to be an immigrant farmer — and even more a farmer's wife. To raise children in isolation, keep clean in a mud hole, and stay warm in subzero conditions was a

First houses on the Prairies were always made of local materials, frequently sod cut from the fields. This rude hut was in Vilna, Alberta.

challenge. To clear the land and pull stumps with the man of the house was back-breaking but essential if a cash crop was to be put in the ground. Then there had to be a garden, whose planting and weeding was the duty of the wife and children. Soon there were cows to be milked, butter to be churned, preserves to be put up for the winter. The job of living was endless and hard. Only the strong survived; only the fortunate prospered. It took courage to leave family and culture behind, to be packed into cramped conditions aboard a ship better suited to the transport of cattle than people, and to venture into the often hostile Dominion of Canada. The hopes and dreams of success and a better life in the "new country" were too often dashed, killed in the slums of the cities, destroyed in the harsh winter of the Prairies, worn down by disease and discrimination. But still people came in the hundreds of thousands.

Living conditions for immigrant workers in the cities were often cramped, as this Bulgarian rooming house in 1912 Toronto demonstrated.

City of Toronto Archives, Health Department Series #58

Sifton had wanted only farmers, but how could he keep out the potential workers and urban dwellers? He couldn't. Conditions were bad in Britain, Italy, Russia, Austro-Hungarian Poland, and the Ukraine, and the most energetic and enterprising looked elsewhere for opportunity. Canada was "the golden land," a place for a new start, a land of opportunity. Many who came were single, or married men who had left their families behind. They aimed to work for a few years to save money towards a small business or a better life back in the Old Country. These sojourners intended to return home; many did, but usually they found that their wages were too low to do more than subsist in Canada. Frequently the family tie withered; too often the workers became industrial accident statistics, killed on the job in a mine, factory, or mill.

In fact, the labour of the immgrants was essential to the prosperity of the dominion. The immigrants were the men who built the railways, as two new transcontinental lines made their way from east to west. They were the men who operated the lathes in Winnipeg's factories or puddled steel in Hamilton. They were the coal miners in Alberta, the fishermen off British Columbia's coasts. Whether Japanese, Croatian, Chinese, or Jew, all these immigrants were labour to be used by Canada's emerging capitalist class. And businessmen wanted immigrants, even setting up offices abroad to compete with Sifton's efforts to bring in only farmers. "Let them all come in," Sir William Van Horne of the Canadian Pacific Railway said in 1906. "There is work for all." The newcomers worked cheaper and often harder than the native-born — something that infuriated the country's nascent labour movement, which wanted higher wages for its members — and they were expendable. If they were hurt, there was usually no family to complain or seek help. After all, as Frank Oliver, Sifton's successor as minister of the interior, said in 1905, they were merely "the off-scourings and dregs of society." Some immigrants, resentful of their treatment, gathered in industrial cells and discussed radical ideas current in Germany or Russia. Such activities only confirmed the Olivers of Canada in their distaste for the newcomers. Why didn't they accept their place and be grateful they had been admitted on sufferance into God's country? Still, the minister was quite willing to accept immigrants' votes once they were naturalized. The newcomers overwhelmingly voted Liberal.

In the cities, the immigrants congregated together into ethnic ghettoes. The Jews huddled around their synagogues, kosher butcher shops, and garment factories. The Ukrainians in North Winnipeg or Edmonton collected near the Ukrainian Orthodox Church. The Chinese had their Chinatown quarter in Vancouver with a population of two thousand, the Japanese their Japtown. These tiny, struggling communities might be foreign in the eyes of established Canadians, but they had life, vitality, a smattering of culture, and an intense desire on the part of their residents to get ahead. School was one way to make it; crime, for a few, was another; and the start-up of a small business — a laundry, a restaurant, a corner store — yet a third.

Newcomers wanted to be with their own kind, to shop for familiar foods in stores owned by countrymen, to speak their own language. The children would find adaptation to Canada easier than their parents did.

National Archives of Canada PA84811

There were always local "fixers" who could negotiate with the civic establishment, delivering votes, once citizenship was acquired, in return for special arrangements, payoffs, and jobs.

Governments provided no infrastructure of services to ease the newcomers' transition to Canada. "The man who will work," Sifton said, "usually makes good and values his success." True enough, but social welfare services did not exist in turn-of-the-century Canada. Government simply did not see unemployment insurance, family allowances, or old age pensions as its responsibility. There were no English or French as a second language classes in schools for children — or adults. Newcomers were left on their own to pick up the Canadian languages. There were no guaranteed rights, no Charter of Rights and Freedoms, no shields against discrimination, no human rights codes. Workers received no protection from exploitative bosses, and single men living in squalid boarding houses no protection from gouging landlords. The immigrants were on their own.

Sometimes, Protestant churches tried to assist. Their settlement houses in the cities provided advice, practical education, instruction in English, and a smattering of Canadianization for mothers and the young. Public health nurses worked with altruism, to be sure, but also in the hope that the spread of infectious diseases could be checked before they reached the middle classes. Teachers in urban schools often took real interest in their charges, spotting intelligent children and trying to help them along. But it was hit or miss at best.

On the Prairies and in mining or lumbering towns, there were no services at all. The immigrant family or worker was completely alone. Neighbours — sometimes five, ten, or even twenty miles away — could help in a crisis, and a cooperative spirit did take form on the Prairies. But language, religion, and ethnicity were barriers that could not easily be crossed. Not surprisingly, many failed, moving off the farm to urban areas or returning to the Old Country. It was a miracle that so many more immigrants stayed, gradually dug a foothold in Canada, and saw their children grow and prosper.

The immigrants were not well treated, whatever their origin. They were ordinarily seen as a lower class of being, and the nation did little to assimilate them or turn them into good citizens. But they succeeded through their own efforts. The reason was simple: Canada really was a land of opportunity, a place where men and women could rise as far as their talents allowed. It was a democracy, a place of freedom. The Ukrainian writer Joseph Oleskow, who offered his *Advice to Galician Emigrants to Canada* in 1895, captured the essential tactic for newcomers: "It is primarily important ... to get rid of the stigma of slavery in the course of the trip [to Canada], to lift your head and look squarely into people's eyes instead of looking from under the brow like an animal chased by dogs. Don't bow and do not humiliate yourselves because if you do, free people will turn away from you in disgust." Act like a free man, in other words, and you will become one. In Canada the immigrants did indeed become free. Even so, the coming of the Great War in August 1914 would test Canada and Canadians, whatever their origins, in ways no one could have foreseen.

CHAPTER THREE

CANADA AT WAR

Courtesy of Department of National Defence

*T*he month of July 1914 found Canadians on vacation. The middle and upper classes found refuge at their cottages or at resorts, those less favoured at municipal beaches or swimming pools. Farmers, of course, had no vacation at all during the short summer growing season. In Ottawa Sir Robert Borden, the Conservative prime minister, packed his bags and headed for Muskoka. The newspapers, for almost all Canadians the sole source of news, were worrying about a crisis in Ireland, where Protestants and Catholics were at daggers drawn. This was an issue Canadians, with their high British and Irish immigrant population, could focus on, if not exactly understand. But, as Canadians knew, the troubles in Ireland had been going on for a century.

At the end of June 1914, the newspapers had reported that the heir to the throne of Austria-Hungary, Franz Ferdinand, had been assassinated with his wife in the obscure Bosnian town of Sarajevo. For the next three weeks nothing much seemed to be happening, so the Balkan crisis subsided in the public mind. Then, suddenly, there was talk of war between Austria-Hungary and Serbia. The dispute quickly spread: the Russians supported the Serbs, the Germans supported the Austrians, and the French supported the Russians. As those Canadians who were interested in foreign affairs knew, this development brought the crisis to the shores of Great Britain.

The British were deeply involved with the French, though how deeply only a handful of ministers and generals in London knew. Sir Robert Borden certainly did not know, but, given the gravity of the crisis by the end of July, he was not surprised to be called back to Ottawa. Most Canadians assumed that, if Britain were involved in a war, Canada would necessarily join the mother country. Foreign policy was a lively subject in Canadian politics, a surprising fact for a British colony like Canada that had, constitutionally, no foreign policy of its own. But Canadians had been self-governing for seventy-five years: they managed their own affairs, paid for their own government, and generally did what suited them best.

When Sir Wilfrid Laurier was prime minister, the country had almost split in 1899 on whether to send troops to join a British war in South Africa. The troops went, setting a precedent. For the next decade Laurier was under constant pressure to do more for defence.

Opposite: The war in the air fascinated homefront Canadians, who spoke of "knights of the air" and "gallantry" almost as if shot-down airmen did not die terrible deaths. These pilots standing around their open cockpit aircraft, with their canes and mascot, probably reinforced the popular image.

It was not that Canada itself was in any particular danger. The United States, Canada's only neighbour, was not interested in attacking a country that so closely resembled itself and that, in any case, was too small in population and too poor, comparatively speaking, to be a rival. Laurier knew that, in a dispute with the Americans, the British would offer only limited help. From that perspective, assistance to the British Empire was a one-way street. In his heart of hearts, Laurier believed that Canadian money was better spent at home than on battleships for the British fleet; but he also knew that most Canadians — the English-speaking variety — did not agree with him. Reluctantly, he authorized a Canadian navy.

In World War I, as in the Boer War, patriotism found expression in song. In this one the German emperor, depicted as a vulture, has been treed by John Bull.

It was not, politically speaking, enough. The opposition Conservatives, led by Robert Borden, charged that Laurier's Liberal government was insufficiently British in spirit and patriotism. When Laurier concluded a trade agreement with the United States in 1911, the opposition proclaimed it to be treason. So did many Liberal businessmen, who feared American competition. Forced into a federal election in September 1911, Laurier lost to Borden in a campaign focused on pro-British sentiment in English Canada and fear of Laurier's navy in Quebec.

The 1911 election offered conclusive proof that English-speaking Canadians thought of themselves as British. If Great Britain were in danger, Canada would be at Britain's side. As for French Canadians, Borden thought he could handle them. Surely in a crisis they, too, would respond affirmatively.

The crisis of the summer of 1914 seemed to show

that Borden was right. Great
Britain declared war on Germany, which had invaded
France and Belgium, on August 4, 1914. Belgium was a
neutral country and Ger-
many had ruthlessly violated
its rights. Germany must be
stopped. Borden's bellicose
minister of national defence,
Sir Sam Hughes, was greatly
relieved. There would be a
war, and the cause — defence
of neutral rights — was just.

Sir Sam set about orga-
nizing for a war that he believed would be short. Canada's professional army was
tiny and had to be supple-
mented. Scrapping existing
plans for mobilizing Canad-

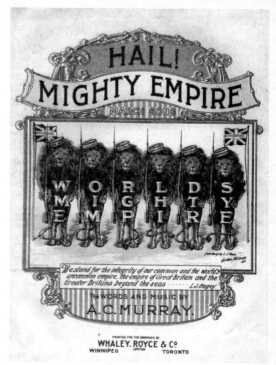

National Library of Canada, Music Division

"Hail Mighty
Empire": The
countries of the
empire — shown
as lion cubs —
rallied to the
British cause.

ian troops, he called for volunteers, organized them into new units
— battalions labelled by number rather than name — and brought
them to a large military camp at Valcartier outside Quebec City.
Over thirty thousand soldiers arrived in August and September,
amid great confusion. After the most rudimentary training, they
were put on board ship, headed for the war. A first Canadian contingent set sail from Quebec on October 1, 1914, arriving in England
two weeks later. It would serve as part of the British Army in
Europe. Canadian troops naturally wore British uniforms and,
equally naturally, were commanded by British generals. No senior
Canadian officers had suitable military experience. Only in 1917
did a Canadian general — a real-estate agent in civilian life — assume
command of the Canadian troops in France.

The circumstances for recruiting were exceptionally favour-
able. For one thing, most of the first contingent was in fact British-
born, closely attached to Great Britain. For another, the Canadian

economy was in a slump in 1914 and there was plenty of unemployment. The army offered an alternative. Finally, in the first weeks of war there was virtually no dissent in either English or French Canada. The British cause (soon called the Allied cause because of the alliance with France and Russia) commanded support from newspapers in Montreal and Quebec City as it did in Toronto or Halifax or Calgary. Sir Wilfrid Laurier offered enthusiastic support from the opposition in Parliament, and even offered sensible advice on the shaping of emergency legislation, the War Measures Act of 1914, to meet the crisis. Borden assumed broad powers for war, making the war in fact as well as in spirit a national enterprise.

Borden, and certainly Hughes, ignored warnings from the professional British general who held the position of Canada's chief of the General Staff, effectively the nation's chief military organizer and adviser. The war could be long, he cautioned, and casualties could be heavy. It was not advice the politicians wanted to hear; unfortunately, it was the most realistic advice Borden got that year.

The war of 1914 — marching and manoeuvres in northern France as the Germans struggled to reach Paris, and the British and French strove to defend it — turned into a war of trenches and mud on the Western Front, the longest line of trenches the world had ever seen, stretching from the North Sea to the Swiss Alps. There was an Eastern Front too (the Russians versus the Austrians and the Germans) and soon there would be fronts in the Balkans and Italy, as Turkey and Bulgaria joined the war on the German side and Italy joined the Allies.

Canadian troops reached the Western Front in April 1915, in time for a German poison-gas attack. The Canadians held their positions, establishing a reputation for toughness and reliability that they maintained for the next three years of warfare. More Canadians soon arrived, as the war continued: a second contingent embarked for Europe, followed by a third. A First Canadian Division was followed by a second, a third, and a fourth, making up a four-division corps — the Canadian Corps of the British Expeditionary Force. Finally, on New Year's Day 1916 Sir Robert Borden announced a new target for Canadian recruitment: an army of 500,000 men.

It was a challenging objective. The total Canadian population was about 8 million, of which half were male. Women were not considered for enlistment, in Canada or anywhere else, since fighting was assumed to be a male duty. Men of military age were a fraction of the male half, and men physically fit to join the army a further fraction. Men were needed to keep the economy going, in a country that was more than half rural and dependent on hard physical labour in farms and forests. An anti-urban bias further distorted manpower estimates: urban dwellers not already in uniform were assumed to be both numerous and "slackers," whose recruitment into the army would be a social good. But unemployment, which had made recruiting easy in 1914, was virtually gone by 1916. Instead, Canadian factories were humming, producing shells and other explosives for the war.

Canadian Defence Minister Sir Sam Hughes (left) and British Minister of Munitions Lloyd George greeting a young woman at a military function in England.

The government in Ottawa understood this complicated situation only imperfectly. It could hardly be blamed: Canada had never confronted such a crisis before and lacked trained administrators. Nothing in the experience of politicians had prepared them either, and they bumbled along as best they could. Sometimes their limits were painfully obvious. Sir Sam Hughes, for example, insisted that Canadian troops in the mud of France should carry the finely calibrated Ross Rifle, a superb instrument for target practice, but woefully insufficient for the mire in which

National Archives of Canada PA206611

the troops actually had to work. The troops abandoned the Ross for the more prosaic but infinitely more serviceable British Lee-Enfield. Borden eventually dismissed Hughes, whose dictatorial technique and administrative incompetence became too much to bear.

In any case, it was not the rifle but the machine gun that ruled the battlefield. Against machine guns and entrenchments, any number of brave infantry charges collapsed. Yet military doctrine, applied by both Allied and German generals, held that the enemy army must be defeated in the field; the war couldn't be won if the enemy's army remained intact. Frontal assault, supported by masses of artillery and tons of shells, was the technique of choice. Casualties rose steadily, and by 1916 the number of reinforcements was not keeping pace, either for the Canadians or for other British troops. Between the summer of 1916 and the fall of 1917, only 2800 infantry reinforcements reached the Canadian Army in Europe.

In the summer of 1916 the British Army attacked the German Army along the Somme River in northern France. On the first day of the battle, July 1, the British Army suffered 60,000 casualties; among them were most of the men from the Newfoundland Regiment, not part of the Canadian forces but, like the Canadians, serving

Canadian casualties being evacuated by a horse-drawn truck in the Battle of the Somme, 1916.

National Archives of Canada PA206612

under British command. Canadian forces took part in the closing stages of the Battle of the Somme, but, for the Canadian Corps, 1917 proved to be the greatest trial.

The campaign of 1917 began triumphantly for the Canadians, who on April 9 swept over strong German positions and took Vimy Ridge, overlooking the French city of Arras. The battle for Vimy Ridge was only a prelude to the main battle, as the British attempted to break through German lines in Flanders, to the north. The battle of Flanders, better known as the Battle of Passchendaele, after a village near the centre of the combat, finally ended in November 1917 when Canadian troops occupied what was left of the town. There was no breakthrough, but there were plenty of casualties: 250,000 on each side, including 15,654 Canadians.

National Archives of Canada PA1596

Sir Robert Borden was, by 1917, becoming distinctly uneasy about the progress of the war. In a short war, or one fought with low casualties or with competent management, British leadership would have caused few, if any, problems. But the war was long, casualties were heavy, reinforcements were hard to procure, and British leadership failed to produce positive results. In 1915 and 1916 Borden became increasingly resentful of what he took to be lackadaisical British direction of the war effort. In 1917, when a new

Mobile soup kitchens brought hot food to the front: Canadian soldiers having a coffee break in August 1917.

British prime minister, David Lloyd George, summoned the leaders of the various British dominions to London to take part in an Imperial War Cabinet, Borden was briefly encouraged. In the face of heavy casualties among Canadian troops, he determined to send reinforcements by force, if they would not go voluntarily. He would enact compulsory military service — conscription.

Borden knew that his government's war record did not command universal confidence at home. There had been scandals over war supplies and discontent in Quebec. French Quebeckers had at first supported the war, not in the same numbers or to the same extent as their English-speaking fellow citizens, but respectably enough. They grew discouraged with an army that spoke English almost exclusively, and with a government that ignored their grievances at home while preaching sacrifice abroad. Moves by the government of Ontario to suppress the teaching of French in tax-supported schools in that province prompted some French-Canadian orators to remark that the real enemy was not just the Prussians (Germans) of Europe, but the "Prussians of Ontario." Borden refused to intervene, calculating he could do little good and might alienate whatever support he still had in Ontario.

Quebec was a problem, so he appealed to his old rival, the Liberal leader and former prime minister, Sir Wilfrid Laurier. He asked Laurier to enter a coalition government with him in the spring of 1917. The Liberals could have half the cabinet, except the office of prime minister, on the condition that they helped enact conscription. Laurier, in one of the most significant moves of his public life, refused. He was firmly committed to the war effort, which he had supported consistently since 1914. He knew that Borden had public opinion in English Canada on his side and that he risked a split in his own party between English and French. But he dreaded leaving anti-Borden, anti-conscription opinion in Quebec without a legitimate voice in politics. Opposing conscription, he forced a general election and divided his party. Most prominent English-speaking Liberals joined the government, and their leaders accepted office from Borden.

The 1917 election was one Borden could not probably have lost, yet his government decided to make sure. It passed a Wartime

Elections Act that disenfranchised any immigrant from an enemy country who had arrived in Canada after 1900. Such immigrants, most of whom had little affection for their countries of birth, traditionally voted Liberal in elections. Close female relatives of servicemen got the vote, for the first time in any federal election, and special arrangements were made for servicemen overseas to vote. Not all these provisions were unfair, but they were calculated to achieve a particular result. Laurier called the act "a blot upon every instinct of justice, honesty and fair play," but most Canadians, caught up in the rightness of the cause of conscription, did not agree. Two weeks before the election, Borden also promised he would not apply conscription to farmers. Farmers were needed to produce food; equally, rural constituencies were needed to produce votes. Not all farmers voted for Borden, to be sure, but, in the final result, self-interest, rural style, was not lacking.

Borden and his coalition government of Conservatives and conscriptionist Liberals won the general election of December 1917, 153 seats to 82, and with 58 percent of the popular vote. Canadians, except in parts of the Maritimes, had voted ethnically: French Canadians (and German Canadians) for the Liberals, Anglo-Saxons and others for the Union, or coalition, government. Conscription was implemented, months after Borden had originally intended, and too late for the opening of the 1918 campaign in France. It was the Germans who led off in March 1918 with a devastating attack on British forces. They almost broke through, and in the crisis that followed Borden decided that he must break his promise to the farmers. Farmers' sons must go to war after all. His decision, impelled by what he took to be military necessity, would prove harmful for the Conservative Party, but only after the war.

The actual effects of conscription were controversial. Enforcement of the draft fell on local authorities. Local boards could grant exemptions, and grant them they did. In parts of Quebec and in farming regions across the country, almost nobody was drafted. In the end, an estimated 47,509 conscripts got to England, and only 24,132 into the lines in France and Flanders.

Borden took the near defeat of spring 1918 to be one further indictment of British leadership in the war. In meetings in London later that season he and other dominion leaders supported Lloyd George in an effort to bring British generals more directly under civilian control, but just at that point the military situation changed. The United States had entered the war in April 1917 and, even though this added player was balanced by Russian withdrawal from the war that fall, American resources in men and money were so immense that they made a difference — a crucial difference as it turned out.

Canadian soldiers relaxing in front of a heavily shelled building in Mons, Belgium, at the end of the war in November 1918.

Toronto Telegram Collection, York University Archives

Courtesy of Maritime Command Museum

Courtesy of Maritime Command Museum

*O*n December 6, 1917, a huge explosion caused by the collision of two ships devastated the great port of Halifax, the wartime starting point for North Atlantic convoys. The blast devastated the working-class north end, and huge fires finished the job. To top it off, a terrible blizzard slammed the shattered city. There were 1600 dead, 9000 injured, and 6000 left homeless. Aid poured in from Canada and the United States, medical care and shelter were improvised, and the war

The harbour to the right

North end looking towards Dartmouth

16

National Archives of Canada PA206614

The battles of the spring of 1918 exhausted the German Army. When the Allies went on the offensive in August, the Germans could no longer resist. The Canadian Corps fought its way through German trenches, as it had so often before, but this time the soldiers broke through the final line and reached open country — trees and green grass instead of shell holes and mud. The Canadians formed the vanguard of the British Army as it advanced into Belgium, retracing the fighting of 1914. The German Army withdrew, fighting, but at the end of October German generals informed their government that they could not continue much longer. The German government must seek an end to the fighting or face certain defeat.

Victory brought pomp and celebration: Canadian generals at a thanksgiving mass in a city in northern France, 1918. Sir Arthur Currie is the general on the left.

The Germans sought a cease-fire, an armistice, which was granted and took effect on November 11, 1918. As the hour of the armistice, 11 a.m., struck, Canadians were still fighting, and long after the end of the war there was still dispute whether the casualties of the last day had not died in vain. Enough were already casualties: 60,000 killed and 172,000 wounded; thousands (2800 as late as 1927) would linger in veterans' hospitals for years after 1918.

At the time, the end of the war met with great rejoicing. In Vancouver the news arrived in the middle of the night, but a crowd of 25,000 assembled at the corner of Granville and Hastings streets, where, according to a newspaper, "self-confident, prim men and women hammered tin cans, blew horns and shouted in glee." Firecrackers went off across the city, and wounded veterans staged a pajama parade. The next day a band toured the city by streetcar, while bagpipers blew their own special contribution to the festivities.

The country needed relief. The war reached into almost every facet of Canadian life. At first, enthusiasm for the war was genuine and the government needed to do little in the way of propaganda. As the war dragged on, the temperature of political oratory went up. Atrocity stories were freely published, demonstrating that it was not just the German government or the German ruling class ("the Junkers" or "the Prussians") who were at fault, but the whole German people ("the Huns"). Hatred of the enemy percolated through Canadian society, resulting in the banning of German language and literature courses in universities. "Disloyal" or "dangerous" foreigners could be rounded up and placed in internment camps.

Full employment and scarcities of goods at home stimulated inflation: wages rose, but not as fast as prices. The government was busy creating money to run the war, and more cash chased fewer goods. Facing scarcities, workers demanded increased wages and organized them-

The home front: the government used posters to remind civilians to save food for the war effort.

We are saving you YOU save FOOD

Well fed Soldiers WILL WIN the WAR

National Archives of Canada C95281

selves into unions to get them. Farmers demanded higher prices, and, because the Allies were short of food, especially wheat, they met with success. To manage the food production and distribution system, Ottawa appointed a food controller in 1917, only to find that the job was administratively impossible. A vast, decentralized country like Canada could not begin to ration food or control prices: the machinery to do it was so large as to be unthinkable — at least to the minds of 1917-18.

The government had already taken a perilous step forward by implementing an income tax in 1917. It could do so in part because the Americans had already done it, and there was little danger of citizens fleeing with their money across the border. The problem, again, was administration. The tax was slow and cumbersome: it took two years for any money to flow into Ottawa's coffers. Instead of paying for the war while the war was on, the tax helped pay for the huge war debt that the federal government had incurred. Income tax, even in the inefficient form that the Borden government had devised, had come to stay.

Income tax signified at least a willingness to contemplate sacrifice. Borden was at heart a reformer, one who believed that the war could improve society by encouraging selflessness among Canadians. To the dismay of Conservative partisans, the government reformed the civil service, putting competence ahead of political loyalty. Reformers had for decades been trying to ban alcohol as a social evil: the war afforded them their opportunity. Starting with Alberta in 1915, every English-speaking province voted to outlaw the consumption of alcohol. Only Quebec held out. In 1918 the Borden government enacted prohibition as a war measure. Some observers believed that prohibition was effective in forcing down the crime rate and, indeed, crime statistics dropped drastically between 1914 and 1918. But, in any society, the group most likely to be involved in crime is young males — precisely the group that had gone to war.

Another change brought about by war, and much noted at the time, was the employment of women. Before 1914 women had a limited choice of occupation. They could work in the home, a job that included repetitive and often back-breaking labour. On farms, women worked even longer and harder. Women had been teachers for decades — half the teaching force in Ontario was female in 1870 — and they could also be nurses. The war and manpower shortages brought women for the first time into factories — 30,000 of them in munitions plants alone by 1918. Women volunteered for farm labour and for a variety of jobs in the city. Men reclaimed many of these jobs after the war, but others they did not. To take one example, the proportion of clerical jobs done by women doubled between the censuses of 1911 and 1921, from 9.4 percent to 18.7 percent, and the number of women in the professions increased by 50 percent.

The prominence of women rose in other ways as well. Women reformers were the major force behind prohibition, and the prohibition movement served as a training school for involvement in other areas of politics. Using arguments based on the sense of community and common sacrifice involved in the war, women got the vote provincially in 1916-17 in Manitoba, Saskatchewan, Alberta, British Columbia, and Ontario. Having got a limited vote for the 1917 federal election, women as a whole were granted the franchise in 1918. Once the Maritime provinces fell into line, only Quebec stood out, as it had against prohibition. It took another war before women in Quebec received the vote, in 1940. The Canadian electorate thereafter included every British subject over the age of twenty-one.

The Borden government placed large hopes on the peace conference the Allies convened in Paris in January 1919. During the war Borden had secured not merely recognition, but consultation from a British government that acknowledged the major role the empire had played in the war effort. Without dominions like Canada, the empire's war effort would have been considerably less, and Great Britain's standing as a world power would have diminished. Borden and a delegation of senior ministers and officials travelled to Paris to join the British Empire Delegation at the peace conference. It had two main purposes, which were somewhat at odds with each other. The first was to make peace in the traditional way, by rewarding the victors and penalizing the losers. By weakening Germany, the Allies and especially the French believed, there would be less danger of aggression in the years to come. The other purpose, strongly supported by American president Woodrow Wilson,

SPEAK!

VOTES FOR WOMEN

Until the war the campaign for votes for women was futile, as this cartoon shows.

Archives of Saskatchewan N-A-369

was to make war itself less likely by providing against sudden crises of the kind that had occurred in July 1914. If possible, the victors should try to eliminate international inequalities, jealousies, and rivalries.

Borden hoped for two things: international recognition for Canada, though not at the expense of its special relationship with the British Empire, and a stable peace to prevent such wars as the one just past from ever occurring again. He had no particular design for the peace, but he hoped he could avoid imposing heavy future commitments on Canada, which, as he reminded the other delegates, had sacrificed so much.

At the end of June 1919 the Allies imposed the Treaty of Versailles on the defeated Germans. The treaty limited German armaments, removed territory from Germany, and permitted the Allies to extract money — reparations — from the Germans and occupy their western fringe. It provided for a League of Nations, where nations would meet, discuss, and, if necessary, enforce international order. There would also be an International Labour Organization, a small bow in the direction of labour and international economic cooperation.

Borden got part of what he wanted. Canada was recognized at the conference and became a founding member of the League of Nations. That appointment in itself acknowledged Canada as a country with international standing, though it also retained its connection to Great Britain. No longer a colony, Canada was on its way to becoming an independent state. Borden was unhappy that the conference committed itself, and the League of Nations, to a peace settlement that, in private, he believed to be unenforceable. But Canada was a small country, the interests of the British Empire were at stake, and a continuation of the war was unthinkable. Canadian troops, still in Europe, were rioting to return home as quickly as possible. Like other delegates, Borden took the peace he could get and went back to defend it.

The country Borden found on his return was in a sour mood, though not unrecognizable. Labour unrest had been mounting in 1917 and 1918, and so had radical union organization. Inflation was impoverishing workers, who naturally were resentful. The government had no effective labour policy: it urged, but did not enforce, fair wages on employers, who had their own interests to consider. In Winnipeg, the Prairies' economic centre, radical unions proposed and actually called a general strike in the spring of 1919. Canada's governments — the City of Winnipeg, the Province of Manitoba, and the Dominion of Canada — responded with alarm. What would happen when Canada's army returned and was demobilized? There had been a revolution in Russia and a communist state had been established. Could there be communism in Canada too? Some of the rhetoric of the Winnipeg strikers persuaded the authorities that the general strike was the first step in a Canadian revolution.

Fearing the worst, and scared above all of their own returning soldiers, the government suppressed the strike and arrested its leaders. The strike collapsed with a puff of air — it had never been as
serious as the authorities believed.

Returning soldiers brought their experiences back to Canada.
Many had been separated from Canadian society for four years.
Often from strict rural and religious backgrounds, they had found
another world in England and France. As Canada adopted prohibition as a war sacrifice, Canadian soldiers learned to drink and smoke
and swear. In some ways these were surface changes, but in other
respects the returning soldiers had a profound impact on the world
they had left behind them. Some Canadians were right to be nervous of what the soldiers would bring and what they would do,
but it was in social rather than political ways that the generation of
1914 altered Canada.

The war was a profound experience for Canada. It was a national experience, as Borden understood it to be. Canadians pulled
together, or pulled apart, over a great national issue, the extent and
meaning of Canadian participation in a terrible international catas-
trophe. There was a sense that Canada had not got it quite right —
that the effort was magnificent, but the result incongruous. A fault
line had opened between English and French Canadians, and
between labour and owners. Party politics had been disrupted, but
the parties were still there. Propaganda had whipped up hysteria
against the enemy and against improbable terrors at home, and, in
the aftermath, Canadians were vaguely ashamed. Canadians had
gained self-confidence, but they did not for the most part draw the
conclusion that they wanted to live apart from Great Britain. Nobody wanted to have the experience repeated, and yet, in a curious
way, the First World War prepared Canadians to do just that.

All these contradictions would have to be worked out — but,
in 1919, not just yet.

THE ROARING YEARS

CHAOTIC TRADING CONDITIONS
WILD IDEAS
TARIFF THEORISTS
CLASS CONSCIOUSNESS
SOCIALISM
FINANCIAL UNEASINESS
WORLD UNREST
SHIP OF STATE

National Archives of Canada C29632

The 1920s were the years of the automobile. Before the Great War, cars were the province of the rich for the most part, extravagances that chugged around the city streets and over the few paved highways in Canada. By the end of the 1920s the automobile, while not yet parked two to a garage at everyman's house, had become the essential means of transportation for the rich, the middle class, and, to some extent, the working poor and farmers.

The numbers alone were striking. In 1914 there were 74,000 motor vehicles registered, of which 45,700 were passenger vehicles. In 1919, the first full year of peace, the figures were, respectively, 342,000 and 196,000. By 1929 the total had tripled to 1.19 million vehicles, of which 1.03 million were passenger cars. In a population of 7 million, there was one car for every seven Canadians — or, roughly, one for every other family. Drivers' licences scarcely existed. When first-time buyers picked up their Ford Model Ts, the salesman gave them a five-minute course on shifting gears. The first trip home was always an adventure.

If cars wanted to travel, roads had to be built and paved. In the cities, where roads had often had dirt or cedar block surfaces into the new century, paved roads kept pace with urban growth. In the countryside, the provincial governments pursued the construction of highways, opening up rural areas to modern conveniences. As the roads spread, so too did gas stations, telephones, and electricity; country folks gained access to urban markets, and city-dwellers easy entrance to vacation cottages in the countryside. The automobile made journeys that had hitherto taken hours, if not days, into short trips. Distance at last was conquered.

So too was the need for privacy. The long-established rituals of courting, the polite dance of young men and women seeking a spouse, were altered forever by the automobile. A teenager could get access to the family car and go to some secluded spot with his girlfriend. There was none to chaperone, none to chastise, none to say "break it up." The car meant freedom, and it fit well into an age of flappers, short skirts, jazz, movies, and cheap illicit booze. The old ways, severely battered by the horrors of the war, were crushed by the ethos of the new decade. The personification of that new ethos was the young man behind the wheel of a roadster with his girl beside him.

Opposite: Arthur Meighen succeeded Borden, leaving Canada in good hands, or so this Conservative cartoonist believed. Canadians disagreed, however, voting Meighen out of office at the first opportunity in the 1921 election and reducing his Tory party to third place in Parliament.

Or, perhaps, the daring young man in his flying machine. The Great War air aces had captivated the public imagination around the world. In Canada, where heroes like Billy Bishop and Billy Barker had abounded, there was huge interest in aviation. At war's end many trained pilots wanted to continue their careers in the air, but the dominion's air force (like its navy and army) was clearly destined to be tiny, ill-equipped, and underfunded. Aircraft were not yet capacious enough to carry many passengers, but surplus aircraft

Like Billy Bishop, many wartime fliers wanted to stay in the air. Most failed in the aviation business.

National Archives of Canada PA1654

abounded and manufacturers were willing to craft pontoons so planes could land on lakes. The bush pilot was born, a distinctively Canadian term for itinerant pilots who flew to isolated areas to ferry in prospectors or carry the sick to civilization. Pilots like "Wop" May developed enormous reputations for courage and daring. In the new Canada, the airplane seemed to fit in perfectly.

If life had suddenly become "modern," there were few signs of it in Canadian public life. In a nation that had a Gross National

Product throughout the 1920s of around $5 billion a year, government was still small, its role circumscribed by the laisser-faire attitudes that said everything should be left as much as possible as it was. The tariff, the duties charged on goods coming into Canada, remained the main source of federal government income. In 1920, for example, total federal revenues were $437 million and expenditures were $529 million; nine years later, revenues were $453 million against $405 million in spending. Income and corporate taxes were relatively tiny. The main charges on the federal exchequer were railways, especially with the Canadian National having to swallow the failed transcontinentals other than the Canadian Pacific, and interest on the national debt, greatly swollen by the costs of the war. What was new as a charge on the state were veterans' pensions and benefits, as the nation tried to repay its debt to those who had fought for it and suffered wounds in body and mind. The veterans complained bitterly that the nation had never rewarded them properly, and their lobby group became an important political fact of life.

Canada's leaders also thought small. Sir Robert Borden's Union government, elected in December 1917, survived the war's end. Borden himself, sick in body and spirit, hung on until 1920, when he arranged the transfer of power to Arthur Meighen, his ablest minister. Meighen was intelligent but blinkered, a man whose logician's mind persuaded him that once he had analyzed a problem, his answer was the only one possible. Meighen also carried too much political baggage: he was the sparkplug behind conscription, hugely unpopular in Quebec and rural Canada; he had created the plan to nationalize the failed railways, which bondholders saw as virtual confiscation; and he remained a proponent of high tariffs, something that angered western farmers. His government also failed to tackle rising unemployment as the wartime economy contracted. Those were four strikes against Meighen, and as soon as the electorate went to the polls in 1921 he was out, his party reduced to third place in the House of Commons with only fifty seats.

The Liberal leader was William Lyon Mackenzie King, grandson of the rebel of 1837, educated with a law degree and a doctorate in economics, who already possessed a good record as a social worker, civil servant, member of parliament, and cabinet minister. King was an expert on the relations between industry and workers, on the need for conciliation, and he had published a book on the subject. Few read *Industry and Humanity*, but at the 1919 Liberal convention that chose him to succeed Sir Wilfrid Laurier, King seemed exactly the man Canada needed. The Winnipeg General Strike was fresh in the minds of delegates, and who better than a young man — King had been born in 1874 — with fresh ideas? King won the 1921 election, holding on to the party's Quebec support and picking up enough seats in English Canada to form a bare majority government.

The fly in the ointment was the Progressive Party, the loosely structured organization thrown up by the nationwide farmers' revolt that took shape during the war. The farmers wanted change, and they captured control of the provincial governments in Ontario, Manitoba, and Alberta. In the federal election of 1921 they elected sixty-four MPs to make their case in Ottawa. Farmers were tired of seeing governments run by lawyers for the interests of the urban rich, the railways, and the banks. They wanted lower tariffs on the tractors and combines they needed and lower prices on everything else. The National Policy that kept out cheaper U.S. goods, they claimed, forced them to buy at high prices from the industrialists of central Canada. They wanted constituency rule and MPs who would do what their voters wanted, not merely follow the dictates of the party bosses. Their leader in Parliament was Tom Crerar, a farmer's

National Archives of canada C29635

organization official and Borden cabinet minister, but essentially a Liberal. Crerar had a frustrating time trying to lead a party that did not want to be led, and he quickly resigned. King had tried to entice him into a coalition in 1921, but failed, something that fed mistrust in Progressive ranks. Even so, for King the main task of his government was to bring the farmers back to the Liberal Party. There would always be a light in the window for them.

Trade and tariffs, especially with the U.S., were always hot political issues. Farmers and workers complained about high prices, while manufacturers demanded protection from "unfair" foreign competition.

The Maritimes were almost as restive as the Prairies. Proponents of Maritime Rights yearned for the days when the region's economy had real heft, but the population was in decline and the agitation for federal assistance was sharp. Maritimers wanted subsidies for their industries, changes in the tariff, and better rail transportation. In the election, one Progressive MP in New Brunswick won office. King was slow to respond to the pressure from the East, but in 1926 he created a royal commission to examine the regional complaints. Railway freight rates were lowered as a result and some subsidies rose. The agitation largely petered out.

That King had even studied the Maritime problem after five years in power was uncharacteristic of the early years of his regime. Virtually everything else King did was marked by a half-step forward and a quarter-step back. His government offered no startling initiatives in domestic politics other than to introduce an Old Age Pension in 1926 for those over seventy years of age who passed a "means" test. Even that small step towards social welfare had been squeezed out of King by the Ginger Group of labour and left-farmer MPs. The government tinkered with the tariff, modified railway rates slightly, altered tax rates a bit, and continued to build post offices and wharves in Liberal strongholds. It was small government by small men in an age of laisser-faire.

King demonstrated the same approach in Canada's dealings with the League of Nations, based in Geneva. The Americans had stayed out, revelling in their splendid isolation. Canada had entered the league because membership demonstrated the new nation's international high standing, earned on the battlefields of France and Flanders. But that was as far as it went. Every effort to give the league some teeth to enforce collective security on a fractious world was met with nay-saying from Ottawa. The league was important, King said — so important that if it hadn't existed it would have to be created — but the gaze of most Canadians remained firmly fixed on their own collective navel. With 60,000 dead, the country had paid a high price for involvement in the Great War. Now, except for

Prime Minister King quickly mastered the art of being all things to all Canadians. This cartoon portrayed his recipe in brilliant style.

a small group of fire-breathers in Toronto and Anglo-Montreal, few Canadians seemed interested in any further overseas adventures.

The one area where King showed some spine was in relations with the British Empire. A convinced monarchist, a believer in the goodness and greatness of the empire, King nonetheless hated being taken for granted by British dukes and generals. He fiercely resented the incident when, in 1922, Britain and Turkey had come close to war, and London issued statements suggesting that Canada backed the British policy, without the courtesy of first asking Ottawa if it did. When the press sought his opinion, King's reply was instinctive: "Parliament will decide." Fortunately, Parliament was not sitting at the time, and King's deliberate stalling, while it infuriated the British, appeared to go over well with those millions of Canadians who wondered why Canada had paid so high a price in the Great War. King understood that foreign policy always posed the risk of dividing isolationist French Canadians and the more imperially minded English Canadians — he had, after all, watched conscription destroy the Liberal Party in 1917. To him, the best solution was to temporize, to delay, to try to increase Canadian autonomy step by step. The objective for King was not independence from Britain, but the end of the automatic obligation to follow wherever British interests went. At imperial conferences in 1923 and 1926, King set out to achieve these ends, and, when the Statute of Westminster finally passed through Britain's Parliament in 1931, he had achieved his goal. Canada had been independent in domestic policy; now it was an independent dominion in foreign policy, too. The nation remained under the British Crown and it was part of what was now beginning to be called the British Commonwealth, but it was independent, or as independent as it wanted to be. Without question, this increased autonomy was the highlight of King's time in power in the 1920s.

The voters did not seem overly impressed. In the general election of 1925, King had been stunned to discover that his government was seen as a do-nothing regime. The Conservatives under Meighen had rebuilt their organization, and the Tory leader, one of the greatest orators in Canada's history, dominated debate in the countryside, exactly as he had in the House of Commons. The farmers were in increasing disarray and, while the Liberals made gains in the Prairies, so too did the Conservatives. The result was stunning: Meighen had 116 seats, against 99 for King and 24 for the Progressives. No one had a majority, and, as was his right, King decided to stay in power until such time as he demonstrated his ability to govern — or not — in Parliament.

Meanwhile, a major scandal involving bureaucrats, thugs, and cabinet ministers had been uncovered in the Customs Department. Parliamentary committees probed, newspapers thundered, and the Progressives, who disliked Meighen more than they mistrusted King, began to waver. King seemed on the verge of a defeat in Parliament when he went to see the governor general, Lord Byng. He had governed for months (though for almost all that time without meeting Parliament), he told Byng, and now he wanted a new election. Byng refused and told King he was going to invite Meighen to form a government. Furious, King resigned on the spot and told the country that Canada no longer had a government.

Meighen quickly set about forming his government. A convention of the day required newly appointed ministers to be re-elected in by-elections, so Meighen appointed a cabinet of acting ministers from among those in his caucus who had previously been privy councillors. He alone resigned his seat — a fatal error, for it meant that the new Tory government was effectively leaderless in the House. The Liberals attacked relentlessly, accusing the government of being illegal because its ministers had not followed convention and resigned. There was some truth in this — Meighen had been too eager to take power, convinced he could finish King off and allow time for the by-elections. On a vote of confidence, the new administration went down to defeat by one vote. Byng promptly gave Meighen the dissolution he had refused King a few days before.

The issue in the 1926 election was less the details of the "King-Byng Wingding," which almost no one except a handful of constitutional experts understood, but a constitutional issue that everyone could comprehend: Who was to rule in Canada — an elected government or an appointed British governor general? King flogged this issue across the land while Meighen vainly tried to relate the delicate negotiations between the two prime ministers and the governor general and focus on the Customs scandals. In essence, voters had

HALCYON YEARS

*F*or well-off Canadians, the 1920s were the halcyon years. The war was over, there were fast cars, money, and everything one could desire, including high-fashion clothes for women. The country's poor, however, suffered from inflation, poor working conditions, and uncertainty for most of the decade.

Illustration by Lorretto Dee, by permission of *Exile Editions*

Still, it was the best of times. Bracketed by war
and the Great Depression, the 1920s are remembered
for their fun, style, and freedom. Nations, like
individuals, need good memories, and if those
memories are not wholly true, it matters to no
one but historians.

Photograph by permission of *Exile Editions*

to choose between the straight and rigid Meighen and the sinuous and clever King. They chose King, and by doing so they set the pattern of Canadian politics for the rest of the twentieth century. It was to be the Liberals who would rule.

Almost unnoticed in the constitutional furore was the virtual demise of the Progressives. The organized farmers movement elected only twenty MPs, while the Liberals won the rest of the seats on the Prairies. The shrewdest political tactician in Canadian history, King had successfully absorbed the farmer revolt by offering just enough tariff reform, just enough nationalism to the West. This was an accomplishment that Meighen, if he contemplated it at all, was forever too stiff-necked to try. As it was, the frustrated Meighen was soon replaced as Tory leader by R.B. Bennett, a bachelor millionaire lawyer and speculator who, with his pince-nez and wing collar, seemed the archetypal Tory.

National Library of Canada, Music Division

Meanwhile, life went on in the best of all possible worlds — or so it seemed in 1920s' Canada. The unemployment that followed the war had been severe — as high as 15 percent — and wheat prices fell rapidly to about half the $3 a bushel they had commanded in 1920. The fall in income hurt consumption, and manufacturers laid off workers in a seemingly endless cycle of despair.

Wartime hero Viscount Byng might have expected an easy ride as governor general. But Canadian politics ensnared him, and he left Canada a bitter man.

By the middle of the decade, however, just as Mackenzie King headed into the 1925 election, conditions improved. Wheat prices were high and new industries forged ahead, as lumber, nickel, other minerals, and hydro power generated huge profits and jobs. Export markets for Canada's products seemed to opening up, and the huge boom in the United States fed the demand for Canadian resources. In the general euphoria, it was easy to ignore the high tariff proponents in the United States Congress, even though one-third of Canada's national income came directly from exports to the south and elsewhere.

One Canadian resource was very much in demand south of the border — booze. In 1919 the United States had imposed prohibition on itself, cutting off alcohol from all but those who had a doctor's certificate. But thirst was near universal, and Canadian fortunes were made by distillers who produced good Canadian rye whiskey and bad imitation Scotch in huge quantities for smugglers to carry over the forty-ninth parallel by boat or truck. The United States government was furious that Canada turned a blind eye on this traffic, and serious incidents occurred on the high seas when Coast Guard vessels intercepted Canadian rum-runners. Ottawa protested, claiming that no Canadian laws were broken by this southbound traffic, but the real beneficiaries were organized crime gangs in both countries. Not that Canadians supported drunkenness. Most provinces were still experimenting with various forms of prohibition, and only Quebec refused to join in the sanctimonious efforts.

National Archives of Canada C128063

Drink bedevilled Canadian life, and in 1920s Quebec the campaign for temperance featured religious imagery.

Indeed, Montreal was the largest, greatest, and liveliest city in the land. It had a night life with clubs, bars, and dance halls unlike the pallid imitations in Toronto, Winnipeg, or Vancouver. It had sin in the form of brothels, and, if other cities had prostitution, Montrealers seemed to carry it off with more style. The restaurants in the city and in the provincial capital of Quebec City were good, something that could not be said of the roast beef and Yorkshire pudding that graced even the most expensive tables in the rest of the country.

Good restaurants required an affluent clientele, and rising wages for many, but not all, fed the boom. Wages overall peaked in Canada in 1920 and did not reach similar heights until the Second World War. Even the steady upward trend through the 1920s was uneven: manufacturing wages were sluggish, mining pay fluctuated dramatically, and the salary of telephone operators remained steady. As always, the prosperity of Canada was not evenly parcelled out.

Even so, new industries created new fortunes. The growth in automobile sales demanded gasoline stations and garages, and men like Charlie Trudeau, the father of a future prime minister, made his money in running a chain of service stations. The birth of radio as an entertainment medium fostered the creation of radio stations and radio receiver manufacturers, most notably Toronto's Ted Rogers, who established the Rogers-Majestic Company and invented an alternating current radio tube that captured the burgeoning industry. But there were problems. The Americans were first in the field with high-powered radio transmitters, and large corporations like NBC tried to capture the Canadian market. Nationalism demanded that Canadian voices should continue to be heard, and the government felt obliged to create the first of countless royal commissions on broadcasting. Ottawa had less success in resisting the flood of American movies into Canada. The "silents" were hugely popular, and Canadians revelled in home-grown talents like Mary Pickford who made it big in Hollywood.

For women, the decade was one of gain. The liberation was not shared by all, of course, and it scarcely existed in rural Canada, where farm wives wore overalls more than short skirts. Even so, there was work as teachers: in 1920 women held 48,000 of the 57,000 teaching positions in Canadian public and secondary schools, at a time when public education was expanding and new schools and collegiates were being built across the land. There were jobs as nurses, telephone operators, and secretaries for those who wanted them, and a limited number of factory jobs were open to women. Some women became lawyers, doctors, and even engineers, though only a few. In 1920 there were 19,075 university undergraduates in all of Canada, of whom 3716 were female; for graduate students, the overall total was an astonishingly low 315, of whom 108 were women. Birth control remained primitive, and the double standard — the woman who sinned was at fault, never the man — continued to prevail. The percentage of illegitimate births, however, was between 2 and 3 percent during the decade, suggesting that abortion, though a crime, was widely practised.

The 1920s at last saw women begin to break into public life. Ontario's Agnes Macphail was the first member of parliament, and Nellie McClung helped win the "Persons Case" that gave women the right to sit in the Senate.

© Canada Post Corporation, 1990/1973. Reproduced by permission.

Labour-saving appliances began to reach into Canadian homes during this decade. The washing machine reduced a tedious chore to one of minutes. The vacuum cleaner, though heavy to pull around, made another household task easy. The electric refrigerator was beginning to challenge the ice box, eliminating the necessity to haul pails of water away. And virtually every home in urban Canada had electricity, a telephone, and indoor plumbing. It would take another two or three decades before the same could be said of farm homes. Middle-class women employed maids — even relatively low-paid civil servants in Ottawa had a maid and a nanny to look after their children. Life was good for those with work, and it seemed to be getting better year by year.

Politically, there were also advances. Women could now vote in federal elections and in all provinces except Quebec, which held out until 1940. They could run for office, and the first woman elected federally was Ontario's Agnes Macphail as a Progressive in 1921. But, anachronistically, women could not be named to the Senate because Section 24 of the British North America Act limited senatorships to "persons" — and women were not deemed to be such. The "famous five," a group of western feminists who demanded full political equality, challenged this interpretation. The Supreme Court of Canada declared that only men were persons in 1928, but the Judicial Committee of the Privy Council in London, the highest appeal court in the empire, overturned that verdict the next year. The committee's decision pronounced the exclusion of women "a relic of days more barbaric than ours." Another barrier had come down for good.

Then there was the stock market — where fortunes could be made in a few days. That they could also be lost just as speedily had not yet entered the public's consciousness. Taxi drivers passed on tips to their customers and elevator operators shared them with friends. It was easy to invest, easy to get rich. Shares of stock could readily be purchased on margin — 5 or 10 percent of the total cost could be put down on purchases. This technique was brilliantly successful if prices continued to soar; it was a disaster if prices fell, for then the brokers would demand payment in full. The makings of a horrific crash were in place.

Singing commercials advertised everything from electric power to sofas — and sheet music, before radio became common, spread the word.

WORDS AND MUSIC BY
WILLIE ECKSTEIN

National Library of Canada, Music Division

CHAPTER FIVE

THE 1930s

Provincial Archives of British Columbia HP 3881

The 1930s were, in most respects, the worst decade of the twentieth century. It was the decade of the Great Depression, a term that applied economically, politically, and even psychologically. It began with the crash of the New York stock market, in October 1929, and continued until the outbreak of the Second World War in September 1939. The nadir was reached late in 1932 or early 1933: to take stock prices as an index — the crisis, after all, symbolically began in the stock market — shares in a company like Massey-Harris, one of Canada's leading manufacturers, declined by 97.4 percent between 1929 and 1932. Abitibi, a pulp and paper company, had shares worth $57.75 in 1929; they were worth $1 three years later.

Opposite: Massive unemployment paralyzed the nation for most of the decade of the 1930s.Unemployed men drifted around the country, easy prey for radicals of the left and right, and begged for spare change.

The Depression affected most aspects of life. Canadians were, on the average, poorer in 1939 than they had been in 1929. In cities they were more likely to be unemployed. If they lived on farms, poor crops and low incomes were a probability if not a certainty. Politically, Canada's leaders spent the decade fighting over shares in a diminishing economic pie. Internationally, Canada began the 1930s at peace and ended the decade in a state of war.

Yet the 1930s were not a uniform experience. Economically, the decade began relatively well in 1929, continued badly from 1930 to 1933, and improved towards the end, between 1934 and 1939, though it never reached the level of the late 1920s. Agriculture and forestry were worst off, while miners were not as affected. Workers in manufacturing industries did better in all but the very worst years of the Depression. Some people actually benefited — prices of daily necessities fell faster than wages. Jobholders, and people with any kind of steady income, consequently did well — as long as they had regular employment.

Threatened by insecurity, most Canadians reacted by clinging to what they already had, or believed they had. Canada began and ended the decade with the Liberal Party in power and with Mackenzie King, that imperishable political durable, as prime minister. In between, from 1930 to 1935, there was R.B. Bennett, the Conservative. It hardly mattered which party was in power, as far as the economy was concerned. Nobody had any idea how to end the Depression. As for what caused it, the only thing politicians could agree on was that it must be outside the country and hence beyond their control.

Meanwhile there was a country to run, and with diminishing resources. Governments, faced with declining revenues, reacted by spending less. The main item in their budgets was the unemployed.

The unemployed were usually depicted as men, both at the time and since. Men sold apples on the street corners in Depression movies. Men stood in breadlines. Women waited at home, sharing the misery but not the status of unemployment. There was something wrong with this picture. Single women, especially young single women, were a significant part of the workforce in cities, where, as an age group, they outnumbered men. Hired reluctantly during the 1920s, they were the first to be let go. In some areas, admittedly, they stayed on — in part because female labour cost less than comparable males.

National Archives of Canada PA168132

The unemployed line up for food outside a Montreal soup kitchen, 1931.

There was no unemployment insurance, and the jobless quickly found themselves on "relief" or "on the dole," grudgingly administered by local governments or private charities. "Relief," interestingly, was different from "welfare." Diagnosed as medically unfit, with possible tuberculosis, one Winnipeg boy was moved from the relief rolls to social welfare. "We thought but little of the change," he later wrote, "until a box of groceries arrived to keep us for a month." Then he was moved to the tuberculosis sanatorium, where it was found that he did not have the dreaded disease after all — but not before he was suitably fattened up. "I made this shattering discovery," James Gray wrote. "As long as I was a broken-down liability to our society, I got lavish attention. Once I was restored to the status of a healthy asset, able and willing to work, nobody wanted me, least of all the Relief Department."

Relief recipients had to prove they truly faced destitution. Cars had to be sold, radios and telephones disposed of, bank accounts emptied. If there was a permit to buy liquor, it had to be surrendered. Then and only then would a deserving welfare applicant be considered. Simply applying was not enough: welfare inspectors checked to see that families were truly penniless. Social controls were even more severe than government regulations: there was a stigma attached to welfare that made the dole not just a misfortune but a disgrace. Individual effort led to success, people believed; individual failure led to the welfare office. Eyes averted, men and women surrendered their privacy and self-respect to get the bare necessities of life for their families. They might, if they were lucky, get $40 a month — and that was in wealthier cities like London, Ontario. In Halifax the figure was $18; in the mining towns of Nova Scotia it was as little as $4.

The manner in which relief was administered added to the general misery. A high-school teacher in rural Alberta noticed one of his pupils coming to school in winter dressed only in summer clothes. The pupil confessed that the relief administrator would not issue him winter underwear because his father was a drunkard. The orders to deny any extra clothing to the boy and his family, it turned out, had come from the provincial capital in Edmonton. After a strenuous protest, the orders were reversed, but only grudgingly.

In Montreal, where 30 percent of the population was on relief in 1932, school authorities found that their charges frequently could not attend classes because they had little or sometimes nothing to wear. The first task of a truant officer was often to secure clothes and shoes for pupils before delivering them to school. Children found to weigh 10 percent or more below the norm for their age got free milk — as long as their parish priest certified that their family was indeed indigent. As a result, only half the underweight pupils actually got the free milk.

Those without families, particularly able-bodied single men, were especially unfortunate. They were regarded with more fear than pity: Would they not take by force what society denied them? It did not happen, by and large, but that did not prevent fear of the unknown. To Canada's political radicals, it looked as if their hour had struck. "To the militant Marxists of the labour movement," James Gray wrote, "the end of capitalism was at hand. Among my father's friends were several who were openly impatient to get on with the business of storming the barricades." It did not happen. Despair and apathy were much more characteristic of the Depression than revolutionary fervour.

The Depression undermined some of the social and economic institutions that had made the 1920s a decade of relative quiet and conformity. Trade unions in the 1920s had been relatively conservative, dominated by "craft" unions like railwaymen or carpenters. Such unions lost credibility and prestige in the face of layoffs and wage reductions in the 1930s. Radical competitors emerged in the form of "industrial" unions that organized whole factories without respect for the different crafts or trades. The industrial unions organized themselves in the Congress of Industrial Organizations (CIO) in the United States, and by the mid-1930s were ready to move into Canada. The radical unions needed organizers, and sometimes organizers were found in the Communist Party, first in the United States and then in Canada. Their immediate target was the automobile industry — centred in Ontario and, by 1936, recovering from the slump and hiring workers again.

Some Canadian governments greeted the CIO with hysteria, particularly Ontario's Liberal government. Premier Mitch Hepburn condemned the union and enlisted special police — derisively called "Hepburn's Hussars" or, more graphically, "the Sons of Mitches" — to protect General Motors in Oshawa against the threat of a CIO strike. Hepburn's frantic activity and extreme language frightened the voters of Ontario — enough of them, at any rate, to get him re-elected in 1937, the year of this confrontation in Oshawa.

The fact that there was a strike in Oshawa underlines the fact that there were jobs in Oshawa and, more generally, in urban Ontario by 1937. To have a strike, there had to be a realistic prospect of winning something, of improving the situation of the workers at General Motors, Ford, and Chrysler — the American-owned "Big Three" automakers. And to have employment, there had to be sales. In fact, there were more cars on Canadian highways in 1939 than in 1929, and more highways too. The Depression was indeed a mixed experience, divided by time, location, and, sometimes, age. It was young men and women, usually but not always unskilled, who bore its brunt.

National Archives of Canada PA205850

Many young men took to the roads and the railways, first searching for work, then looking for food and a place to sleep at night. They did not usually seek opportunities for crime or try to foment revolution. Gangster movies imported from the United States gave respectable audiences a small chill, but gangsters were rare in Canada. Much more fearsome was the vision of communist revolutionaries, inspired by Russia. In Regina the RCMP asked for and received 300 bayonets and 30,000 rounds of .303 ammunition in 1931. They would be ready for a revolution that never came. True enough, there were some communists and some would-be revolutionaries, but their actions, when there were enough of them to act, were pathetically ineffective. If the authorities got wind of protest

Education did not stop, even in the Depression: Frontier College operated in the North in a railway boxcar, 1930.

marches, they were banned. In Vancouver in April 1935, a group of unemployed occupied and vandalized the Hudson's Bay Company store, then marched on City Hall. There Mayor Gerry McGeer read the Riot Act, had the leaders arrested, and ordered the police to disperse the demonstrators. The police battled the rioters and, within a few hours, order prevailed. The mob, if mob it was, went home.

The authorities, from Vancouver to Halifax, continued to be nervous. They had laws against vagrancy at their disposal, providing for the imprisonment for six months of those found wandering without visible means of support. But imprisonment cost money, and cramming the indigent into cells might actually turn the penal system into an auxiliary relief service. The answer had to be found elsewhere. Believing that concentrating the unemployed in urban centres was dangerous, officials used relief allowances to induce single males to go to farms or work camps that were, if possible, located far from cities. Some young men were sent to camps in national parks, but more were dispatched to work camps run by the army. Inmates of the army relief camps received 20 cents a day, room and board, clothes if necessary, and a tobacco allowance. In return they worked on public works projects — highways or airstrips, or anything else that government engineers could devise. To maximize the number of men working and to minimize their own costs, work-camp supervisors ignored labour-saving machinery and relied on pick-and-shovel work. The motivation for this decision was understandable, but the effect on inmates' morale was predictable. To them, even useful projects were degrading and futile make-work. Not surprisingly, the camps became breeding grounds for discontent. A large camp at Long Branch outside Toronto was so unruly that all seven hundred inmates were discharged and sent home.

Most Canadians found it hard to believe that their native-born fellow citizens would stoop to revolution, but they were not so sure about recent immigrants. The authorities seemed to agree: they deported no fewer than 28,000 foreign-born men and women between 1930 and 1935. In case there were any revolutionaries left, the federal government outlawed communism, and Communist Party leaders were sent to the penitentiary. That may have suppressed the political difficulty, but it did nothing for economics. There is an ironic footnote to the communist scare of the 1930s. Massey-Harris, the farm machinery maker that was seen as a symbol of Canada's manufacturing prowess, found itself operating at 10 percent of capacity in the early 1930s. Suddenly it got a shot in the arm — a $6 million order for tractors from the Soviet Union. The company gratefully took the communists' money.

The problem, even for those who regarded unemployment as an individual responsibility, was that there were so many unemployed and so many on welfare. How could all of them be blamed? In Montreal, according to one estimate, 87 percent of working-class families were on relief. Not all of them could be slackers. In 1933 Prime Minister Bennett learned that 32 percent of Canadian workers were unemployed. Worse still, they remained unemployed. There had been depressions before — in 1913, in 1920 — but they had not lasted long. The Depression of the 1930s just kept going. Even in 1938, a year of relative recovery, the unemployment rate was 16 percent.

If anything, these figures understated the crisis. As far as Canada's statisticians were concerned, people on farms were fully employed. In terms of hours worked, that might have been the case, but in terms of income earned, farmers often made as little as the urban unemployed. The crisis began early on the Canadian Prairies, with a fall in wheat prices in 1928. The next year, however, the wheat crop was a disaster, and throughout the 1930s the situation went from bad to worse. In 1928 a farmer could hope to harvest 23.5 bushels of wheat an acre; in 1937 the yield was 8.1 bushels per acre.

Farmers, especially on the Prairies, needed help. Unfortun-

With the wheat economy near collapse, Canada hosted a World Grain Exhibition in Regina in 1933.

© Canada Post Corporation, 1933. Reproduced by permission.

ately the provincial governments were ill-equipped to give it. Their revenues were dwindling, and by the mid-1930s most of Canada's provincial governments were not far from bankruptcy. Help, if help there was, must come from Ottawa. The federal government gave

*C*anadians needed distraction, and the birth of the Dionne quintuplets, the world's first, to a poor French-Canadian family near North Bay, Ontario, certainly provided it. The country and the world showered "the quints," five little girls, with gifts — in this case, clothes and a car. According to the newsreels, the Dionne girls lived a fairytale life;

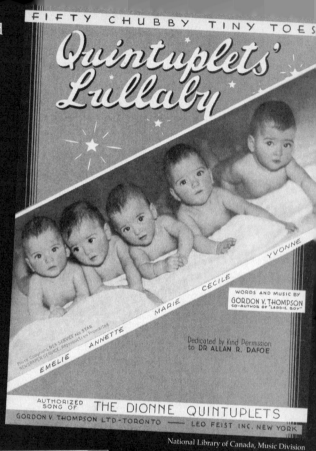

National Library of Canada, Music Division

reality seems to have been much grimmer, and their lives after childhood do not seem to have been especially happy.

two kinds of aid. It handed out money to the provinces to save them from repudiating their debts, which would affect the credit of the whole country. It also gave the provinces help for relief, and some of this money eventually trickled down to farmers.

Ottawa could do nothing at all about the weather. On the Prairies, month after month and year after year, the sun shone, the wind blew, and the rain did not fall. The early settlers had tempted fate, planting crops in areas with marginal rainfall and neglecting to cultivate trees against the wind. Across the middle of North America, from Texas to Saskatchewan, the soil dried up and turned to dust. As the wind blew, it picked up the soil and eventually deposited it along whatever obstacle it found. Driving across Saskatchewan in 1936, a Winnipeg reporter found buried fences along the road. Visibility in the dust-laden air was practically zero on some days, and the sun was darkened at noon. "We drove through village after village without a sign of life," the journalist wrote, "past empty farm after empty farm."

Rural poverty was not confined to the West. In Ontario the 1930s were almost a lost decade where farmers were concerned. The gap between farm life and city life failed to close, or at best closed very slowly during the 1930s. Electricity was installed in some rural areas, and items such as telephones became more widespread. In certain parts of the province, farmers earned so little cash that they reverted to barter. A country doctor reported in 1934 that his payments the previous winter included "over twenty chickens, several ducks, geese, a turkey, potatoes and wood."

Per capita incomes for small businessmen and professionals declined 36 percent between 1928 and 1933, and some doctors, depending on location and clientele, were especially badly off. Ethically bound to provide medical care to those in need, many doctors frequently got nothing for their time and service. Not surprisingly, medical associations began to promote socialized medicine as a solution to their problems. If the patient could not pay, they reasoned, why not the state — the city, the province, or the federal government? In Winnipeg, in 1933, doctors actually withdrew their services while demanding payment for medical care for relief recipients. They pointed out, not unreasonably, that the city paid for groceries and rent for those on relief, so why not for medical services too? But governments recoiled before the prospect of direct intervention into health care. The expense and the extent of the service were bound to be heavy, and new commitments were not what governments wanted.

There was one practical change for the better: governments were not as shy of regulation as they were of providing new services. Tuberculosis was common in Canada as in other countries in the 1930s; highly contagious, it was the dreaded "white death." Every large city had its sanatorium, to which tubercular patients were sent to recover or die. Isolation was practically the only available prevention. There was one other measure — pasteurization, or the boiling of milk — since tuberculosis was known to spread through milk from infected dairy herds. But governments had been afraid to offend the farmers' lobby, and nothing was done. Finally Premier Mitch Hepburn, himself a farmer, did what nobody else dared to do: he ordered pasteurization in Ontario. The dairy farmers, facing the loss of their markets, fell into line.

How did Canadians explain the Depression? It seemed obvious at the time that the Depression came from outside the country. World prices for wheat, lead, and zinc, and American prices for pulp and paper, fell and kept on falling. Politics, in Canada as in the United States and elsewhere, dictated a response: raise tariffs while devaluing the national currency, so as to secure a competitive advantage in foreign markets and deny foreign sellers a market in Canada. Since everybody did it, and Canada's economy was a relatively small part of world trade, this political strategy proved ineffective — except where it was simply disastrous.

There was a second level of explanation for the Depression. According to this analysis, it was a failure of capitalism and, more broadly, a failure of business. Pre-Depression Canada, like the United States, celebrated the accomplishments of modern business, especially the deeds of the large corporation. Large banks, stores, and factories all pointed the way to an orderly and prosperous future, a future of mass employment and many big employers. Canada had large banks, fortunately stable, sitting in high towers in downtown Toronto and Montreal. Canada had large stores, Eaton's and Simpsons, with Eaton's dominating the mail-order market across the country. Canada had big companies — Inco in nickel, Stelco in steel, Massey-Harris in farming machinery — and of course the big automakers General Motors, Ford, and Chrysler. In the 1920s these corporations were the engines that drove the economy. In the 1930s the engines seemed, often enough, to need repair.

In 1934-35 a royal commission, ironically appointed by R.B. Bennett's Conservative government, investigated sweatshops and price gouging by Canadian companies such as the Eaton's department store chain. Canadians were shocked to learn how little they paid their employees and how great their profits were on items made in sweatshops. Obviously something needed to be done — about gouging as well as unemployment. Convinced that unfettered capitalism could not survive, the millionaire Bennett announced a series of reforms in 1935 modelled on the contemporary American New Deal of President Franklin D. Roosevelt. Unluckily for Bennett, he had taken five years to reach this conclusion and, even more unfortunately, an election was due. In denunciations from both the left and the middle of the political spectrum, Canadians condemned Bennett's reforms as deathbed repentance. Right wingers gave their political contributions for the election to the only possible alternative, the Liberal Party led by Mackenzie King.

Prime Minister Mackenzie King, in his winter furs, greets a young admirer in 1939.

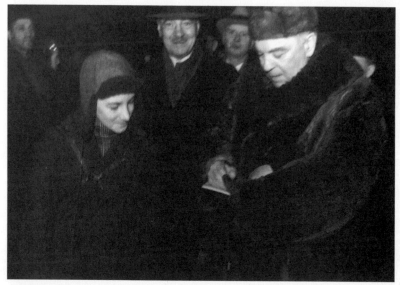

Pudgy and
verbose,
Mackenzie King
was a cartoonist's
delight. Robert
LaPalme's
cartoon catches
the prime minis-
ter's spirit in the
mid-1930s.

National Archives of Canada C42324

"It's King or Chaos," the Liberal election slogan proclaimed. Bennett went down to a landslide defeat in October 1935. King became prime minister again, and Bennett soon slunk off to England, where he became a viscount and a member of the British House of Lords. He died, alone with his millions, in England in 1946.

Mackenzie King had no idea what to do about the Depression. A trained economist, he knew enough to know that he did not have the answer. He believed that nobody else knew either, but he observed that, in small increments, things were indeed getting better. There were fewer unemployed in 1936 than in 1935, and fewer still in 1937. There was a setback in 1938 — an economic downturn, but not a deep one. It seemed that Canada, like the rest of the Western world, was settling in for an indefinite future of high, but not intolerable, unemployment and slow growth.

King had an agenda, carefully crafted for what he believed were very limited economic resources. The economy puttered along, producing more taxes than before, but not enough to allow the government to do anything rash (which King interpreted to mean big). So King tinkered with the structure of government, rationalizing smaller departments into larger departments (Transport, for example). He legislated a government airline, Trans-Canada Airlines, since he did not trust private enterprise to bring air service to the whole country from coast to coast. Business, or private enterprise, was in a low state with public opinion, and its objections could easily be overridden.

King also knew that provincial governments were the other big losers, politically speaking, of the Depression. In British Columbia, leading businessmen appeared before a royal commission to suggest that the provincial government be abolished as wasteful and useless, and its powers given to Ottawa. That point of view was extreme, but it resonated across the country. Canada might be small, and in the face of the worldwide crisis perhaps too small, but it was the biggest thing Canadians had. Small wonder that Canadians began to think of the Ottawa government — always called the "dominion" in the 1930s — as their surest protector.

Ottawa's domestic prestige grew for another reason. The 1930s were a disturbed decade in international relations not merely economically but politically. The First World War had left unfinished business — a dissatisfied Germany, a revolutionary Russia, an expansionist and resentful Japan. Politically the United States chose to sit out the 1920s and 1930s, preaching a message of peace and virtue, but refusing to come up with action to match its words. Starting in 1931, Japan, economically weak but militarily powerful, set out to overthrow international order in the western Pacific. Its target was its neighbour China, which was in no state to defend itself. In a series of wars between 1931 and 1937, Japan encroached on China. The West raised its hands in horror and its voices in condemnation, but did nothing. Convinced that the West would never do anything, Japan launched a full-scale war in China in 1937. In Canada, Chinese citizens and their sympathizers met the Japanese aggression with an economic boycott, but its effects were symbolic only.

The West stayed out of Asia in part because there was another, equally grave, crisis in Europe. To Great Britain and France, a European crisis was much more threatening to their interests and their survival. Germany, the most powerful nation in Europe, was at the centre of the crisis, so the danger was immediate and possibly extreme. In 1933 Germany had elected Adolf Hitler to be its head of government. As an extreme nationalist, anti-democrat, and anti-Semite, Hitler promptly clamped a dictatorship on Germany and organized its resources for war.

Canada had its own Nazis, the tiny Parti National Social Chrétien (PNSC). Many of its members would spend World War II in internment camps.

Mackenzie King was well aware that events abroad posed great peril for Canada. He had participated as a young politician in the controversies over reciprocity (relations with the United States) and the navy (relations with Great Britain) in 1911. He had lost his

National Archives of Canada PA108054

parliamentary seat that year, and had failed to regain it during the conscription election of 1917 that bitterly divided English and French Canadians, and farmers and city dwellers. War, King concluded, was something English and French Canadians were unlikely to agree on, and it was an issue that again could divide, if not ultimately destroy, the country. Given the situation in Germany, King believed as early as 1936 that war was more likely than not.

King would have preferred that there be no war. He refused to encourage the British, who asked him to establish factories in Canada to produce arms. King's response to that and other requests was lukewarm. King had a large and influential parliamentary delegation from Quebec, and he knew that French Canadians did not want a repetition of the Great War, with its conscription and its excited and racially divided politics. At the same time, he knew that English Canadians, far outnumbering the French and ethnically more than half the total population of Canada, would not allow him to stand idly by if Great Britain went to war against Germany.

National Archives of Canada PA107943

Anti-Semitism in Canada: a bilingual sign warning Jews not to visit Ste-Agathe, Quebec.

National Archives of Canada PA129610

Recruiting began in 1939 as soon as war was declared: an artillery unit scouts for volunteers in Montreal.

In terms of domestic politics, King had one great advantage. The British government did not want war either, and it made this view known on every possible occasion. When Hitler advanced, Great Britain and its ally, France, retreated, hoping that Hitler would be "appeased" and settle down. Some in the British government actually believed in this compromising; others hoped to take advantage of the delay before Hitler finally provoked war by rearming. The overall effect was that, however foolish British policy proved to be in deterring aggression in Europe, Canadians became convinced that, if war came, it was because of Hitler, not Britain. And so Mackenzie King slowly increased the budget of Canada's tiny armed forces, publicly held his peace, and waited. He knew that if and when Hitler attacked, Canada would be at Britain's side and in another European war.

Canadian soldiers initially trained in World War I tanks, shown here outside Camp Borden, Ontario.

City of Toronto Archives SC266-61431

It was not something he wanted to contemplate and, given the ruin and economic devastation that the Depression had wrought on Canada, it is hard not to sympathize. In the summer of 1939 Canada faced an uncertain future, but, thanks to Mackenzie King, it faced it more united than anyone a few years earlier would have believed.

ROYAL VISIT

*I*n the spring of 1939 King George VI and Queen Elizabeth visited Canada, the first visit by a reigning monarch. They were rapturously greeted from coast to coast as the Royal Train made its way from the Atlantic to the Pacific. Naturally, Prime Minister Mackenzie King (shown in the photo just behind the royal couple) accompanied the king and queen. It was the "society" occasion of the decade, but it was also a political event: it reminded Canadians on the eve of war of their ties to Great Britain.

CHAPTER SIX

THE SECOND WORLD WAR AND ITS AFTERMATH

National Archives of Canada C87124

*I*n August 1939, exactly as twenty-five years before, Canada was on vacation. The unemployed, the families on relief, the millions living in the poverty induced by the Great Depression might not be lolling by the lake and enjoying the evening breezes at the cottage, but they, too, tried to enjoy the all too brief Canadian summer.

If they read the newspapers or saw the headlines, all Canadians knew war was coming. How could they not? The Japanese were running amok through China, waging a brutal conquest. Italy had conquered Ethiopia, and Il Duce, Benito Mussolini, continually made bellicose noises at his neighbours. In the Soviet Union, Joseph Stalin's communist regime had waged class war against its own citizens and, stunning the world, had struck an alliance with Germany in the last days of August. That seemed to give Adolf Hitler, the Führer of Nazi Germany, a free hand to attack Poland. The Nazi propaganda drums, skilled at mobilizing German opinion and cowing the democracies, had been focusing on the Warsaw government's alleged sins for months. After watching Hitler swallow Austria and Czechoslovakia, no one could doubt that the Poles were next.

The difference this time was that Britain and France had pledged to use force to resist any German attack on Poland. Since the Statute of Westminster had given Canada independence in foreign policy, British action would not automatically bind Canada. But opinion in Canada, while far from unanimous, favoured action, especially in English Canada. On September 1 the German *Wehrmacht* crossed the border into Poland and, three days later, their ultimatums rejected by Hitler, Britain and France declared war.

During the 1920s and 1930s Prime Minister Mackenzie King had repeatedly declared that "Parliament will decide" questions of war or peace. He was as good as his word, summoning members and senators to Ottawa for an emergency session. The cabinet was united in support of war at Britain's side, and there was near unanimity in the Commons. Several Quebec MPs would have preferred the country to remain neutral, and the leader of the Cooperative Commonwealth Federation, J.S. Woodsworth, spoke against war. But the die was cast, and, on September 10, the Dominion of Canada declared war on Germany.

Opposite: Trying to make the best of the disaster at Dieppe in August 1942, the government released this poster showing Lieutenant-Colonel C.C.I. Merritt of the South Saskatchewan Regiment winning a Victoria Cross by rallying his men on the French coast.

There were clear understandings in Parliament and across the nation on how the war was to be fought. The prime minister spoke of a war of "limited liability," in effect stating that Canada was not a great

City of Toronto Archives 64673

Above: Norman Rogers, Lapointe and King led the war effort in 1939-40.

Opposition in Montreal was directed by Mayor Camillien Houde, here addressing an anti-conscription crowd in 1939.

power and was not prepared to exert itself to the extent it had in the First World War. Moreover, King and his Quebec lieutenant, Ernest Lapointe, had made it clear that the government would not implement conscription for overseas service. This war, they said to secure Quebec support for the conflict, would be fought differently from the earlier one.

The strategy worked. Quebec media and politicians acquiesced in the decision to fight. The Québécois understood that the English-speaking majority supported participation

and that opposition to war would provoke domestic conflict. The government's guarantees seemed satisfactory — but not to Premier Maurice Duplessis. Calling a snap election in Quebec for October 1939, Duplessis charged that Ottawa was using the war to centralize its control. Federal ministers from the province entered the battle, pledging they would resign if Duplessis won and promising again there would be no conscription. The provincial Liberals swept the province. The next challenge, from a wholly different direction, came in Ontario, where Liberal premier Mitch Hepburn complained that Ottawa was doing nothing to win the war. Mackenzie King used this criticism as an excuse to call a snap election of his own, and he swept the nation, winning a huge majority. The simple truth was, in early 1940, from Prince Edward Island to British Columbia, there were few who pressed for a large war effort. The 60,000 dead of the Great War, the enormous material, financial, and human costs of that war, were too well remembered for any segment to show enthusiasm for another conflict.

The government moved methodically to create a military force. The regular forces, numbering only 10,000 all told, began the tasks of mobilization. The militia and the air and naval reserves were called up, and volunteers began to enlist. In effect, Canada was completely unready for war. Aside from a handful of modern destroyers, there was no modern equipment — no tanks, no machine guns, no aircraft, no minesweepers. Army volunteers trained in "civvies," sometimes carrying broomsticks, while the government rushed to place contracts for uniforms, rifles, and other supplies. A few aircraft came from the still neutral United States in the week between the British and Canadian declarations of war. Because of American legislation they could not be flown into Canada, so they were literally towed across the border. If ever a nation was unprepared for war, it was Canada in 1939.

The government's idea was that the air war was the critical theatre of operations. When the British suggested that Canada become the centre of air training for the British Commonwealth, Mackenzie King was delighted. The costs would be large, but surely there could never be horrific casualty totals from fighting in the skies. There were difficult negotiations over money and control of the British Commonwealth Air Training Plan, as the scheme came

Canada trained 130,000 aircrew during the war. At Manitoba's Virden Flying Training School, pilot hopefuls learned on the Link trainer.

National Archives of Canada PA140658

to be called, but, by December, the deal was struck. The British even agreed that this plan would be Canada's major contribution to the war. Signed on King's sixty-fifth birthday, the BCATP deal was the embodiment of a limited liability war.

But Hitler and Germany were unwilling to conform to Canadian or British ideas of how the war would be fought. After Hitler's quick conquest of the Poles, the "phony" war lasted until April, when Norway and Denmark were seized. In May the *Wehrmacht* struck at neutral Belgium, Holland, and Luxembourg and then kept rolling into France. In a matter of weeks a humbled France was suing for peace, and the British Army, defeated in the field but still resisting, had to be rescued by fleets of small boats and the Royal Navy from the beaches of Dunkirk. The Canadian Division in Britain had been shipped to France *after* Dunkirk as part of an effort to form a new defence line; fortunately, the hopelessness of the military situation was realized and the Canadians pulled out before meeting the enemy.

In Ottawa the new war situation stunned the government. The unthinkable had happened: Britain could be defeated. The Royal Navy could fall into German hands and, if that occurred, North America might be threatened. Gradually, King and Lapointe prepared the nation to do more. A National Resources Mobilization Act, permitting conscription for home defence only, was pushed through Parliament; a national registration of men and women took place; controls were introduced on scarce materials; and plans were laid for rationing. Recruiting stepped up for all the services, and every aircraft, ship, and trained soldier — few though they be — was rushed to Britain to help defend the "home country," as many still called it.

Canada itself was in danger for the first time in the twentieth century. No longer could Britain, its back to the wall, be counted on to defend it. Rather, Canada had to help defend Britain. In August 1940, when President Roosevelt called Mackenzie King to suggest a meeting, the prime minister was eager. Here was the chance to get American help for the defence of Canada, the essential prerequisite for Canada to be able to mobilize itself fully to support Britain.

The result of these discussions was the Permanent Joint Board on Defence, a committee of generals and officials to report to the two governments on the measures necessary for the defence of

North America. Roosevelt suggested the "permanent" nature of the board, and King accepted it willingly. Although some in Canada complained about the new relationship, and British prime minister Winston Churchill grumbled bitterly to King, the critics were wrong. The board let Canada act to help Britain, confident that its homeland was secure. Still, the balance of power in the world had shifted dramatically in a few months and, for the first time, Canada was now part of the American sphere.

The country's mobilization proceeded at full speed. Home defence conscripts received their call-up notices and reported for training, first thirty days long, then ninety, and finally for the war's

Shipyards, like this one at Victoria, BC, built warships for the first time. HMCS *Edmundston*, a corvette, hit the waves in 1941.

National Archives of Canada PA170287

116

duration. Volunteers poured in increasing numbers to the Royal Canadian Air Force to learn to fly at the BCATP training stations scattered across the land from the east to the west coasts. The RCAF's 250,000 personnel flew in every theatre of war, flew every type of aircraft, and contributed hugely to victory. The BCATP itself produced more than 130,000 aircrew — a massive effort of incalculable value. Meanwhile, Prairie boys joined the Royal Canadian Navy, eventually 100,000 strong, and, after too few weeks' training, found themselves in the North Atlantic on a corvette fighting Nazi U-boats. Their captains were often schoolboy yachtsmen, but most of them eventually learned their trade. By the end of the war, the RCN had convoyed half of all the merchant ships across the North Atlantic. Canada's armies also took form: eventually there were five divisions and two brigades of tanks overseas, while home defence divisions in British Columbia protected the west coast after Japan entered the war in December 1941. By 1941-42 women had won the right to enlist in the air force's Women's Division (WD), the army's Canadian Women's Army Corps (CWAC), and the navy's Women's Royal Canadian Naval Service. The WDs, CWACs, and Wrens took men's places in every aspect of the war but combat. In all, 1.1 million men and women put on uniforms during the Second World War — an astonishing contribution from a nation of just 11 million, and vastly greater than the number in the First World War.

CWACs performed every duty but combat. Here a firefighting team show their stuff in a demonstration in bombed-out London in 1943.

Quebec's contribution to the war effort also was much greater than in the earlier war. Although there was strong support among intellectuals, *nationalistes*, and the clergy for Marshal Pétain's fascistic Vichy regime in France, and although Mussolini's Italy remained much admired in the province, there was also support for Britain's resistance to Hitler and for General Charles de Gaulle's Free French movement. What-

National Archives of Canada PA37479

ever the troubled state of public opinion, some 150,000 francophones served in Canada's armed forces, more than three times the number who enlisted in the earlier war. The army took care, as it had not in 1914-18, to establish infantry regiments other than the Royal 22e, and there were also French-speaking artillery units. The air force had its Alouette Squadron of fighters as well. But it was still an English-speaking military, one that fought and ran unilingually, and very few Québécois rose to high battlefield commands. No francophone commanded a division in action, for example, though Ottawa desperately searched for French-speaking officers capable of rapid promotion. This imbalance caused substantial resentment, but the great fear in Quebec remained conscription.

There was growing pressure for compulsory overseas service in English Canada, especially after Arthur Meighen became Conservative leader for a second time in November 1941 and after Japan entered the war the following month. As the pressure for conscription increased inside his cabinet, King decided to call a plebiscite in April 1942 to release him from his promise against conscription. Instantly, Quebec erupted. La Ligue pour la défense du Canada was created, led by the intellectual journalist André Laurendeau and the viciously anti-war newspaper *Le Devoir*. At their side were the old *nationaliste* élite, ranging from the ancient Henri Bourassa to the quasi-fascist Abbé Groulx, but they were also joined by a host of young firebrands like Jean Drapeau and Pierre Trudeau. King was asking all Canada to break the promise against compulsory service he had made in 1939 to Quebec, the Ligue and its friends charged, and the federal government's weak campaign could never get untracked in the face of that unassailable truth. Limited liability had gone by the board as the war unfolded in Hitler's favour; now, in Quebec's view, conscription was similarly about to be imposed for a war that many in Quebec refused to accept as necessary or just. In the end, English Canadians voted massively to release the government from its pledge while French Canadians voted equally heavily *non*. The government duly amended the National Resources Mobilization Act to make overseas conscription possible, but, in his most famous phrase of the war, King laid down the government's policy: "Not necessarily conscription but conscription if necessary."

The definition of necessity was left unclear, but, for the moment at least, the policy of no overseas conscription remained unaltered, much to the disgust of many English Canadians.

The plebiscite did not disrupt the war effort, however much it angered Quebec. The home-front efforts were extraordinary. From a Depression-wracked economy that had left huge numbers of the workforce unemployed at its worst, Canada moved (with apparent seamless efficiency) to full employment by 1941. Indeed, with so many in uniform, the shortage of labour was profound. Men and women left the farms to work in shipyards, aircraft plants, and factories. Non-essential jobs were eliminated and non-essential industries were obliged to switch production to war matériel. The heavy hand of the state, guided by a much swollen civil service and directed by "dollar-a-year" men

EVERY CANADIAN
MUST FIGHT

National Archives of Canada C87139

loaned from industry to C.D. Howe's Department of Munitions and Supply, told business and labour what to do. To change a job or to move from city to city, everything required the state's permission. Rationing, priorities, organization — nothing looked much like peacetime Canada.

Wartime Canada mobilized as never before as the state controlled the economy tightly.

But people liked it. First, the cause was just, the need was obvious, and most Canadians wanted to help win the war. At the same time, wartime pay was good — the average salary approximated $25 a week — and there was as much overtime in war factories as individuals could want. Gasoline might be scarce, tires unavailable, and civilian automobiles out of production, yet, so long as there was a black market, most people were relatively unaffected. Despite rationing, most Canadians had better food during the war than they could afford during the Dirty Thirties. There was enough meat, butter, and coffee, and although people carried ration books and meat tokens, the inconvenience was far less than Canadians feared. Women coped without silk stockings, but nylons were beginning to make their appearance and other devices — painting a seam up the back of a brown-tinted leg — were adopted. There were even movies on weekends, dances, and the semblance of normal life.

If they over-run Canada your money'll be useless...

Buy VICTORY BONDS *now*

UNDERWOOD ELLIOTT FISHER LIMITED *makers of* UNDERWOOD TYPEWRITE

City of Toronto Archives SC488

To run the war cost billions, and fearful Canadians bought Victory Bonds every year.

Daily, children went to school and sang "God Save the King" and "Rule Britannia." They read war poetry and followed the campaigns on maps. Out of class they traded their dad's cigarette cards showing aircraft and ships, and saved quarters for War Savings Stamps exactly as their parents purchased Victory Bonds. High-school boys marched — usually out of step, in cadet corps, and university students joined the Canadian Officers Training Corps for more serious training. Youngsters swallowed their vile-tasting cod liver oil to stay healthy, collected milkweed pods for sailors' lifejackets, saved tin foil from cigarette packs, recycled Mom's tin cans, and carried cooking fat and bones to the grocery store to be rendered into reusable oils and gelatin. Everyone who could planted a

The war mobilized adults and children. Everything was recycled, and "Canadian whites," uncoloured comic books on cheap paper, created fictional heroes for kids.

Victory garden and made preserves for the winter. Families with sons and daughters overseas worried day by day, but they wrote cheerful letters and sent inexpensive cigarettes by the carton. Magazines were read, then recycled for "the boys" by post. It was almost normalcy — though parents, spouses, siblings, and children lived in fear of what might happen to their loved ones overseas.

The fear was justified. Canada itself was largely spared direct enemy attack. After Japan entered the war and some 2000 Canadian troops were killed or captured at Hong Kong, the 22,000 Japanese Canadians living on the west coast were evacuated inland. The federal government,

National Archives of Canada C46350

War against Japan raised fears in BC. In early 1942, the federal government began to move Japanese Canadians inland, seizing their property, and dividing families.

and particularly the government and citizens of British Columbia, were concerned about their loyalty and their safety from attack by their neighbours. This reaction was rough justice at best, but, at the beginning of 1942, when a brutal Japan was running amok through the Pacific, few Canadians objected. Japanese submarines attacked a lighthouse on Vancouver Island's Estevan Point, and, although a Canadian brigade participated in the American-led campaign to liberate the Aleutian Islands off Alaska, that was the extent of warfare on the west coast. The scenario might have unfolded very differently, however, had the United States Navy not won the Battle of Midway in June 1942.

On the east coast, there were no direct German attacks on coastal points. Still, the U-boats roamed freely in Canadian waters, sinking vessels off Nova Scotia and Newfoundland and in the Gulf of St. Lawrence. The dead washed up on Gaspé shores, bringing the war home. The RCN had to learn the complicated tasks of anti-submarine warfare, and the losses were high until it did. One U-boat even landed in Labrador and established an automatic weather station that beamed signals to Germany. It remained undiscovered until the 1980s, long after the war.

It was overseas that the main ground and air wars were fought. In the skies, the RCAF played its full part. One squadron of fighters participated in the Battle of Britain in 1940, but, as the BCATP poured forth its pilots, navigators, bombardiers, wireless operators, and other aircrew, Canadian squadrons multiplied along with the numbers of RCAF men who served in Royal Air Force squadrons. The major contribution was No. 6 Bomber Group, a massive force of Wellington and Lancaster bombers that carried out attacks on occupied Europe. Stationed in Yorkshire, far removed from target cities, the squadrons suffered heavy losses and had a reputation for indiscipline until a tough commander, Air Vice Marshal "Black Mike" McEwen, took over in 1943. McEwen whipped the group into shape, and it won a formidable reputation for its effective attacks against Germany. Still, air losses were high, with more than 17,000 dead. Mackenzie King had not anticipated the scope and scale of the air war when he signed Canada up for the BCATP.

No. 6 Bomber Group was the RCAF's major contribution to the air war against Hitler. Higher casualties than anyone had expected resulted, as the bombers faced night fighters, anti-aircraft guns, searchlights, and radar. But the bombers inflicted terrible devastation on Germany.

Courtesy of J.L. Granatstein

Nor had he or anyone expected the savagery and heavy casualties of the ground fighting. After the disaster at Hong Kong, the Canadian Army's next day in action came on August 19, 1942, at Dieppe in France. Some 5000 men from the 2nd Canadian Infantry Division and a few British and Americans hit the beaches at the defended port in an attack intended to demonstrate the problems of mounting an invasion of Europe. There were immediate problems: surprise was non-existent; the supporting flotilla's guns were too few and too weak to make much of an impression on the Nazi defences; the tanks that made it to shore through the surf could not make headway on the small stones that made up the beach; and the enemy's weapons on the cliffs dominated the landing areas. Despite the best will in the world, the Canadians were crushed, trapped in positions in which there was neither cover nor escape. Those who landed were killed, wounded, or taken prisoner, and only a handful made it off the beaches. No objectives were taken in the blackest day of the war for Canada's army. Much of the young manhood of Windsor, Toronto, Montreal, southern Saskatchewan, and Calgary was gone in a few hours.

The infantryman's war was brutal and often short. These soldiers move cautiously along an Italian street.

Photographer Ken Bell, National Archives of Canada PA114482

There was more hard fighting to come. In July 1943 the 1st Canadian Infantry Division and a tank brigade joined in the Anglo-American invasion of Sicily. The campaign was relatively short but brutal, and the troops and their commanders learned how to fight the skilled troops of the *Wehrmacht*. The invasion of mainland Italy followed hard on the heels of Sicily and, by December 1943, the 1st Division was on the outskirts of Ortona, a small Adriatic town heavily defended by Nazi paratroopers. The fighting to take the town was vicious and prolonged, as the Canadians "mouseholed" their way from building to building and both sides blew up houses belonging to the other. Over Christmas, as fighting continued, companies were pulled out of the line for a dinner that would become a last supper for some. Finally, the Germans left, leaving the exhausted Canadian troops in command of the rubble, their division effectively rendered non-effective. "Little Stalingrad," the newspapers called it, referring to the great battle the Russians had waged since June 1942 to hold the city on the Volga against Hitler. As the costly war in Italy went on, Canada's troops increased to a corps at the end of 1943. They showed their mettle in cracking the Hitler and the Gothic lines in 1944.

The Canadians, British, and Americans at last landed in Normandy on June 6, 1944, to open the "second front" that the Soviet Union had demanded as a way of easing pressure on its embattled armies. Canada's contribution on D-Day was substantial: it provided one of five seaborne divisions; a parachute battalion; more than a hundred ships of the RCN; and countless squadrons, pilots, and aircrew of the RCAF. The armed forces had come a long way from the ill-trained regulars and untrained reservists of 1939.

The fighting in Normandy, and later, was bloody and costly. The Canadians first struggled with their Allies to break out of the beachhead, then faced heavy and effective resistance as the First Canadian Army tried to close the Falaise Gap and trap the retreating German defenders. The army next moved eastward along the Channel coast, reducing a number of German fortress cities. By October 1944, after Canadian units had reached the River Scheldt, General Dwight Eisenhower, the supreme commander, gave them their hardest task of the war: to clear the Scheldt estuary so that the

Painting by T.C. Wood, Canadian War Museum 10544

On June 6, 1944, Canadians landed in Normandy, a scene captured in war artist T.C. Wood's graphic *Beach at Courseulles.*

great port of Antwerp could be used to supply the final advance. In dreadful conditions of cold, mud, and water, the Canadians complied, suffering heavy casualties. Regiments died on the Scheldt, as their reinforcements were too few and too poorly trained to provide much strength to the depleted ranks.

The resulting casualties, added to those suffered in Normandy and those still being incurred in Italy, provoked the conscription crisis Mackenzie King had struggled to avoid since 1939. It was not that men were lacking, only that trained infantry were too few. The army reinforcement system had expected fewer foot soldier casualties and more rear area losses, and it proved unable to be flexible, now, when the ratios altered. By October 1944 the shortage of infantry was projected to be 16,000 men, and the only source for this large number lay in the home defence units of conscripts, the "Zombies." As the prime minister desperately tried to avoid the inevitable, he fired his pro-conscription defence minister, J.L. Ralston, and appointed in his stead General Andrew McNaughton, a supporter of the volunteer army. But by mid-November the numbers were unassailable: the Zombies had to go to war overseas. King acquiesced, though he was concerned about Quebec. The newspapers thundered, there were desertions from his caucus, some conscripts went AWOL (absent without leave), and others even staged a small mutiny at their camps in British Columbia — but still there were no great riots in the streets of Quebec. Québécois could understand that King had tried to resist the inevitable as long as possible and that he had won himself few friends in the rest of Canada in the process.

Defence Minister Layton Ralston, here in Britain in 1940, pressed Mackenzie King for conscription. Concerned for Quebec and national unity, King resisted as long as he could. In November 1944, he fired Ralston, but he was soon forced to send home defence conscripts overseas.

National Archives of Canada PA132649

As it turned out, the army overseas was out of action from November 1944 until February 1945, and the casualties of the autumn were mostly made good. Few conscripts made it to the front, and the I Canadian Corps joined the First Canadian Army from Italy in late February. At last, all Canada's army was together under the command of General Harry Crerar. Although fighting was fierce in the crossing of the Rhine and in the liberation of the Netherlands — there are more than 5000 graves in the two main Canadian military cemeteries in Holland — the war wound down to a Nazi capitulation on May 7, 1945. The Canadian Army had lost more than 17,000 men in action, and the total number of Canadians killed during the war was 42,000.

National Archives of Canada PA138353

Fighting on German soil in early 1945, the Canadian Army suffered heavy casualties. This view of Canadian equipment mired in the Hochwald mud suggests the scale of the war.

The war had obliged Canada to come of age a second time in the century. The nation's growing strength was reflected in its massive war effort, and its sorrow was etched on tombstones across Europe and Asia. The new muscle was reflected in the country's power in the world. Despite being a small country, Canada had produced the globe's third largest navy and fourth largest air force, along with a powerful army. The country gave away billions of dollars in food and war matériel to its allies, and its factories produced 10 percent of all British Commonwealth production. That was power, and it purchased respect in the councils of the nations.

Although Canada did not claim a place at the great powers' strategy sessions, it argued for its voice to be heard in those areas where it had special influence. In the production of food and minerals, for example, or the provision of relief supplies to a war-ravaged world — here Canada was a great power and here its diplomats skilfully parlayed the power won on the battlefields and the factories and farms into influence. Britain and France had to be pushed into giving Canada its due place, but pushed they were. By war's end, a new phrase had come into use — middle power — and Canada had earned its position as the first among the middle powers. This recognition mattered as Canada sought to build a sense of pride and nationalism among its people.

For most citizens, however, the war's end meant simple normalcy. The boys would come home, rationing would end, and perhaps a family's accumulated savings could be used to buy a car or a small bungalow. But would there be jobs? Or would the Depression resume its paralyzing grip on the land? Many feared the worst, and the public servants in Ottawa prepared plans to fend off unemployment. In 1940 Canada had created an unemployment insurance system, deliberately doing so when employment was high so money would be in place to cushion the expected post-war slump. In 1944 a scheme of family allowances, designed to put readily available money in the hands of mothers, passed through Parliament, to begin the next year. A huge plan of veterans' benefits, called the Veterans Charter, aimed to reward those who had fought and help them get re-established, educated, and set up in business or on a farm. There was money to help businesses retool for peace and to build new housing, and plans for a great scheme of public works to soak up unemployment.

When the victorious armies finally returned, Canadians rejoiced. The Ontario Regiment, an armoured unit, returned to a celebrating Oshawa, Ont., in late November 1945.

City of Toronto Archives 100525

These preparations helped mightily in the re-election of Mackenzie King and the Liberals in the general election of June 1945. The Cooperative Commonwealth Federation, which in 1943 had led in the opinion polls, suddenly lost its support, while the Conservatives, whose commitment to social reform and the welfare state seemed suspect at best, went nowhere. Even the *nationaliste* Québécois, who had hoped to capitalize on grievances over conscription, found that peace, combined with King's political skill, left them with little room. The government majority was narrow, but, at a time when Britain's Winston Churchill was being rejected by his ungrateful electors, it was amazing for King to win at all.

In fact, the government deserved to win, both for the war effort it had mustered and, amazingly, for the smooth transition from war to peace it engineered. The great crash never came, and soldier and civilian alike made the change to peace with confidence. The country's Gross National Product had doubled to $11 billion between 1939 and 1945, and it continued to grow. Somehow Canada had become the land of prosperity it was always supposed

Would there be jobs for demobilized servicemen and women? The government offered extensive benefits (from education to business grants and farms) to vets and provided much paternalistic advice. In fact, the system worked superbly because the economy continued expanding into the peace.

National Archives of Canada C49434

to be. People found new jobs, had money in their pockets, and relished the chance to raise a family and buy a home. Governments had plans, too, along with the funds to implement them. Business had markets at home and, with the world in ruins, abroad as well. Canada's golden time had arrived.

But there were, as always, problems. The Soviet Union had been the mainstay of the war against Hitler, but the communists remained deeply antipathetic to the democracies. Soviet spies were unearthed in Ottawa, of all places — civil servants, military officers, and scientists who betrayed their oaths and turned wartime secrets over to Moscow. This duplicity stunned Canadians, as did the general bellicosity of Russian representatives at the new United Nations. The war was scarcely over before the Cold War began.

In this atmosphere of fear and apprehension, the nations of Western Europe were in difficulty. Their economies shattered by the war and their societies torn by dissension between right and left, France, Italy, and the Low Countries were effectively bankrupt by 1947. Britain had borrowed $5 billion from Canada and the United States, but that money was being used up fast. What was needed was American aid, and, in 1947, American Secretary of State George C. Marshall proposed a plan to allow Europe to get the dollars it needed to buy the goods it required. Canada did not need Marshall Plan aid — it was rich and prosperous — but it was running out of the scarcest commodity of the postwar years: American dollars. The Marshall Plan gave Canada the way out. Through "off-shore purchases," European states could buy Canadian goods and pay for them with Marshall Plan dollars. The Americans had agreed to help bail out Canada and, for its part, Canada willingly helped bail out Europe with its goods. The ties between Canada and its neighbour were getting ever closer.

Closer ties were still to come. The Soviet threat immediately compelled the European and North American democracies, victorious in the war against Hitler, to consider how they could resist the tide of Soviet communism. The Marshall Plan revivified European democracy, providing the economic will needed to resist the siren song of Marxism. The North Atlantic Treaty, negotiated in 1948 and signed on April 1, 1949, offered the defensive sinew and the power

Photographer Ken Bell, National Archives of Canada PA205851

The bountiful harvest of the Prairies fed the wartime Allies and the hungry of the postwar world.

The able Louis St. Laurent became King's choice to succeed him, and in 1948 the Quebec lawyer became prime minister.

of North America necessary to resist any attack. The United States had the atomic bomb and the economic power, and, with the establishment of NATO, it showed it had the will.

For Canada, it was unheard of to join a defensive alliance in peacetime. What would Quebec say? In fact, Quebec was benign in its attitude, seeing atheistic communism as a danger to be feared. Moreover, Mackenzie King, the man who had presided over Canada's transformation into an independent nation that was both rich and powerful, had gone by late 1948. His successor was Louis St. Laurent, the secretary of state for external affairs. A Québécois, St. Laurent had been a corporate lawyer before coming to Ottawa to replace Ernest Lapointe as justice minister in late 1941. He had made his mark at once and quickly became the prime minister's most trusted colleague and natural successor. Sharing few of the isolationist and anti-British

National Archives of Canada C22720

THE ASBESTOS STRIKE

*U*nder Quebec's Premier Maurice Duplessis, labour unions and strikes were scarcely tolerated. Most of the Roman Catholic Church hierarchy routinely sided with the government, as did business and the media. But a few years after the Second World War, the climate slowly began to change.

Montreal Star

Montreal Star

Montreal Star

Montreal Star

Montreal Star

Montreal S[tar]

Montreal Star

In February 1949, the asbestos workers went on strike at Asbestos, Que., pitting 5000 men against the company and the government, but this time the church supported the workers. So too did union organizers such as Jean Marchand and a young lawyer named Pierre Trudeau. Duplessis nonetheless used tough tactics of mass arrests and police power to intimidate the workers. The archbishop of Quebec City intervened to broker a settlement after four months.

shibboleths of his compatriots, he was brilliantly lucid, politically courageous, and uncompromisingly anti-communist. The world had changed, Canada had changed, and St. Laurent was willing to lead his people — all his people — into the North Atlantic Treaty Organization. "With this Prime Minister," one English-speaking minister said to a journalist friend, "we can do anything."

In 1949 it seemed so. Canada was richer than anyone could have dreamed a decade before. The country's diplomats were listened to with respect and the country's goods were sought after in the marketplace of the world. Canada and Canadians had weathered the storm of Depression and war, and the future seemed boundless in its possibilities.

Canada took in thousand of British refugee children during the war. In a world of shortages, bombing, and death, the dominion was an oasis. Many of these children would return as immigrants after the war.

City of Toronto Archives 107194

CHAPTER SEVEN

THE
SPACIOUS
DECADE

Photographer Ken Bell, National Archives of Canada PA206301

O ptimism and anxiety flavoured the 1950s. The promise of
Canada seemed, finally, to be fulfilled. The economy
"boomed" and expectations "soared." Every year Canadians
seemed to be better off; every year the statisticians confirmed that
that was so. The population rose from 13.5 million in 1949 to 17.5 million in 1959 — up 29.6 percent, the largest increase in a single decade
in Canadian history. On March 31, 1949, Newfoundland joined
Canada, bringing an additional 345,000 citizens into the fold and
completing the country's territorial expansion. The Gross National
Product rose, more than matching the surge in population: at $16.8 bil-
lion in current dollars in 1949, it reached $36.8 billion in 1959. (In con-
stant dollars, using dollar value in 1971 as a base, the GNP moved
from $31.4 billion to $51.7 billion, a rise of 65 percent.) Simply put,
there were many more Canadians by 1959 and they were a great
deal better off.

Canadians took a fair amount of satisfaction in their accomplishments. Pride in Canada and confidence in its future as a nation
characterized public discussion in the 1950s. And why not? Employment was high, inflation was low, and taxes were going down. Everywhere they looked there was progress: new schools, new roads,
new airplanes that were made in Canada, and new houses for the
children of Canada's baby boom. All this and apparently stable values, too, for the 1950s were, for most Canadians, a time of certainty:
new churches dotted the suburbs, and the school day began with a
prayer. In bookstores — though there were not very many of them
— *The Power of Positive Thinking* challenged readers to think well of
themselves and their prospects.

Yet Canadians in the 1950s were not entirely at ease. Overshad-
owing the prosperity of the decade was the spectre of war. Canada
was firmly a member of the Western camp in the Cold War, con-
fronting and competing with the Eastern or Communist Bloc. Both
camps had nuclear arms, and nuclear arms had the potential to ex-
tinguish or even exterminate the populations of countries many
times the size of Canada. Understandably the major item in federal
budgets throughout the 1950s was defence, but, increasingly as the
decade wore on, Canadians were uncertain whether anyone or
especially any government could actually defend them.

Opposite:
The war brides of
the forties had
matured into the
matrons of the
fifties. The
*Canadian Home
Journal* tried to
show that being a
housewife could
be both stylish
and fun.

Courtesy of Maritime Command Museum

In the Cold War, radar stations guarded against Soviet bombers.

This uncertainty was a reminder that there were problems with Canada's size. Geographically, Canada was immense, but in terms of population it was still relatively small — 13 million to the Americans' 150 million. Canada's Gross National Product was good news for Canada and for Canadians' standard of living — second in

A joint American-Canadian command, NORAD, coordinated the air defence of the continent. Here a Canadian officer gazes at a thankfully empty radar screen.

Courtesy of Maritime Command Museum

the world, after the United States. In the nuclear age atomic bombs cost money, and the cost of defence far surpassed what Canadians could afford. Affordability was not confined to defence. Canada could make anything in the world, according to C.D. Howe, the minister of trade and commerce. "Clarence [Howe] always used to tell me that we could grow bananas in Canada," his cabinet colleague Douglas Abbott remembered. "But who would want to pay the price?"

Canada was an importing nation that exported largely raw materials or semi-processed products, such as pulp and paper or lead and zinc. Canadians imported oranges, iron ore, and petroleum to keep healthy, to make steel, and to power their automobiles. They made automobiles too, but in small numbers for the domestic market. The factories that made the cars were owned in the United States — Ford, General Motors, and Chrysler, corporate immigrants from an earlier generation. A small number of Canadians in the 1950s worried about American ownership, as they sometimes worried about the United States in general: so big, so rich, so close, and, though they did not often say it, so tempting. Canadians did not need a passport to visit the United States and they did not need a visa to immigrate there: there was no quota for Canadians.

In some senses Canada and the United States were isolated in the 1950s. It was still difficult to get to North America from Europe, and more difficult still to reach American or Canadian shores from South America or Asia. Although European travel was gradually becoming more common and more affordable, since North American currencies were strong, citizens of Canada and the United States most often visited each other. In an age before widespread air conditioning, the north woods promised genuine physical relief from city heat. The majority of Americans lived in the north or northeast anyway, those parts of the United States that were physically, culturally, and economically like Canada. And so, every summer, Canadians saw incoming caravans of American tourists.

Canadians also visited the United States. Many had relatives there — Canadians were the third largest "ethnic" group — and many more went to shop. The United States not only had more products than Canada but they were cheaper too, made for a much larger market. The Americans had bigger cities, bigger highways, and bigger stores. The Canadians were protected by a high customs tariff, which they regularly tried to circumvent in frequent trips to Boston or Buffalo, Plattsburgh or Seattle. So Canadians bought in the United States, officially or unofficially, and continued the tradition of smuggling that was as old as the border. They knew what to buy because they could watch the advertisements on American television.

The 1950s was an age of gadgets, and the gadgets in turn reflected not so much advances in technology or science as in production and marketing. Television, for example, had been around since the 1920s, and there had even been television broadcasts before the war in London and New York. Only after the war did television sets become affordable and available, however, and only in 1948 did the Americans start broadcasting regular TV. It began in

Television was the cultural event of the fifties, and a bonanza for Canadian retailers.

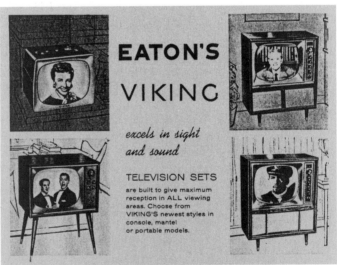

National Library of Canada, Music Division, Vancouver Symphony Orchestra Program, Oct., 1959

the big cities on the east and west coasts, and reached the Canadian border around 1950. Soon TV sets, huge wooden boxes with 8-inch screens, appeared in Toronto or Montreal. It was easy to see who had them, since they needed high, ungainly metal aerials to pull in the American signal.

The Canadian government surrendered to the inevitable. The Canadian Broadcasting Corporation would provide Canadians with television; otherwise, it was clear, they would take matters into their own hands and watch American programs. To a Liberal government jealous of Canadian autonomy and fearful of an American cultural invasion, it was obvious that Canadian TV must provide a counter-attraction — a Canadian voice and image. In 1952 CBC broadcasting began in English and French, in Toronto and Montreal, and moved across the country — to Ottawa , Vancouver, and Halifax via the CBC, and to Sudbury, Hamilton, Regina, Saint John, and other places via private stations.

Photographer Henry Fox, National Archives of Canada PA206751

Television wanted to be everywhere: a CBC "portable" camera unit from 1959.

Television became such a mass-market phenomenon that it is interesting to recall how expensive it was in the mid-1950s. Mid-range TVs cost $400 or more — perhaps 10 percent of a middle-class family's income. The audience that watched TV could afford to watch TV, and early television earnestly tried to be up-market. The CBC in the 1950s regularly produced plays from the English-language canon, from Shakespeare to Christopher Fry. The broadcaster also recognized that this was Canada and that Canadians liked sports: it routinely broadcast the two Canadian teams, the Toronto Maple Leafs and the Montreal Canadiens, in the National Hockey League, itself a six-team enterprise confined to the American Northeast and Midwest, where winters were long and fans understood an ice-bound game. For years Canadians had heard about Maple Leaf Gardens in Toronto and the Forum in Montreal; now they could see them.

In the spring of 1955 Canadians saw hockey in another light entirely, faithfully broadcast on television. The star player of the Montreal Canadiens, Maurice "the Rocket" Richard, was suspended for the rest of the season by the president of the NHL, Clarence Campbell. Richard had indeed seriously offended against hockey's rules, but his suspension doomed the Canadiens' hopes just as they were going into the playoffs. When Campbell attended a Canadiens' game, Montreal fans took matters into their own hands. Campbell fled, and the crowd, by then a mob, spilled out onto the downtown streets, breaking shop windows and looting. The police stood by. At the time, commentators treated the event as just another lawless outbreak; but it was also true that most of the rioters were French Canadian, and relatively poor, and most of the victims were English-Canadian businesses.

Hockey was not the only sports phenomenon of the 1950s. Football had existed in Canada since the 1870s; some enthusiasts plausibly argued that the game in its modern form, a development from rugby, had been invented in Canada. But the game was better played, or at least better financed, in the United States, and, from the 1930s on, Canadian football teams had imported players from south of the border. Over time, football teams became city rather than university or club based. By the 1940s, therefore, local pride was often bound up with the local team. Since the early 1900s Canadian teams had competed for football supremacy, symbolized by the Grey Cup, a trophy donated by a governor general in 1909. Gradually the Grey Cup became the object of east-west contention, as eastern teams played western teams for the football prize. In 1948 the Grey Cup game between the Ottawa Roughriders and the Calgary Stampeders caught national attention. Football, hockey's poor and distant relative, began to catch on, and throughout the 1950s the Grey Cup game became an occasion for national festivities. The American players on Canadian teams in what became the Canadian Football League in 1958 balanced the Canadian players on American teams in the NHL. Baseball in this period in Canada was still a minor league enterprise, and the principal Canadian teams served as farm clubs for the big American teams.

Hockey and football became staples of Canadian visual entertainment. Still, between drama and high culture at one end of the

By permission of *Exile Editions*

TV spectrum and sports at the other, there was a vast middle ground dominated by American or American-inspired programs. In the first category, at 8 o'clock every Sunday night in the Eastern time zone, there was the *Ed Sullivan Show*, live from New York. Sullivan presented a kind of TV vaudeville that ranged in content from Senor Wences, the ventriloquist-comedian, to Elvis Presley, the pop idol, to the Canadian comedy team of Wayne and Shuster. There were pre-recorded programs like *I Love Lucy*, with the comedienne Lucille Ball and her Cuban husband, Desi Arnaz. Canadian-produced, but American-inspired, shows included *Space Command*, which even by the undeveloped standards of the time was ludicrous, and *Trans-Canada Hit Parade*, featuring songs performed by local talent.

Television had a noticeable social impact. Residential streets emptied when favourite shows came on, and nothing could be seen from outside but the silver flickering of the TV sets. Because several popular programs were scheduled around the dinner hour, some families ate "TV dinners," foil wrapped and pre-cooked from the supermarket, on "TV tables." Social critics pondered these developments and quoted the American broadcast regulator, Newton Minnow, on the "vast wasteland" of network television.

Television in the 1950s was not an all-day affair, especially in areas serviced only by the CBC. During the day only the radio was available, to cater to an audience presumed to consist almost entirely of housewives. Men went to work and women stayed home, or so the legend had it. That was not strictly true, although the labour force was overwhelmingly male (77 percent) in the 1951 census. It was difficult to find a man on residential streets between 9 a.m. and 5 p.m., except for servicemen and the elderly. The 1950s were the swan song of the old urban institutions of the "breadman" and "milkman," who delivered their product daily from door to door.

It helped that unemployment through the decade was relatively low, 2.8 percent in 1949 rising to 3.4 percent in 1956 and, abruptly, to 7 percent in 1958. There was a brief recession in 1953-54, the only one of the decade. Popular legend has it that there was another in 1958, but, while unemployment rose that year, the economy as a whole did not shrink. The federal government ran surpluses most of the time, amounting to 15 percent of total revenue between 1948 and 1953, and 7 percent between 1955 and 1957. The surpluses were justified as an inflation-fighting device, and inflation, though a problem in 1949-52, dropped and remained very low for the rest of the 1950s. Stable prices, lowered taxes, and rising incomes made for an unusually contented electorate.

In June 1949 Canadians re-elected the Liberal Party under Louis St. Laurent with a record majority, 193 out of 262 seats in the House of Commons. With St. Laurent they had one of the most competent governments in Canadian history, one already schooled in the problems of peace and war. The Liberals knew that their support rested on the contentment of the citizenry and that Canadians wanted an improved standard of living. Housing was one item people wished to buy.

The Liberals had made sure the electorate was better housed. The federal government under Mackenzie King enacted legislation to make mortgages more available to homebuyers. The result was more buyers and more homes. Canadian cities moved outwards as suburbs resumed their march. In Montreal the suburbs moved west across Montreal Island, creating the "West Island," a district populated by affluent English speakers, and south across the St. Lawrence.

In Toronto, growth urbanized the townships immediately adjacent to the city, which caused the provincial government in 1953 to create "Metropolitan Toronto," a federation of the city with its immediate suburbs. Soon suburbanites outnumbered the citizens of the core city, which in fact lost population as its inhabitants moved to new houses.

The federal government's mortgage program encouraged the construction of houses that met centrally approved standards. As a result, a distinctive Canadian style of house spread across the land — not universal, but pervasive enough to be recognizable from St. John's to Victoria. The distinctiveness lay in the details, not the concept: Canadian suburbs looked like American suburbs, another source of grievance for Canada's nationalists. The better suburbs incorporated features designed to make them superior to the cities they surrounded — curved streets, dead ends with turning bays, and larger lots that allowed space between houses and greater privacy. Some suburbs incorporated small shopping centres, an importation from the United States and an alternative to the time-consuming trip downtown. The first shopping centre in Canada was the Norgate project outside Montreal, built in 1949, followed by Dorval, also near Montreal, and Northgate, in West Vancouver, in 1950.

Most new housing was detached, single-family dwellings. The trend reached a peak in 1958, when 105,000 detached houses were built, though apartments that year were beginning to catch up, at 47,000. Into these houses Canadians packed large quantities of electric refrigerators, washing machines, and clothes driers — and, starting in the mid-1950s, dishwashers. Where Canadians dwelled, they liked to own, and federal policies encouraged the trend, making Canada a country of owner-occupiers. The trend applied everywhere but Quebec, where renters were still the majority.

The 1950s also witnessed the completion of trends that dated back to the 1870s. The 1951 census discovered that 886,000 Canadian homes had no indoor plumbing of any kind — taps or toilets. There were houses without electricity too. These dwellings were mostly in the country, but not for long. Except for the most isolated areas, Canadians were connected to hydroelectricity by 1958 (4.2 million

NEW CANADIANS

*T*he 1950s were a period of steady, large-scale immigration, almost entirely from Europe. Great Britain, the Netherlands, Germany, and later Italy contributed hundreds of thousands of "New Canadians." Even the British found life strange, for North America in the 1950s was an island of abundance in a world of scarcity and rationing. Central heating, supermarkets, and spreading suburbs meant an ease of life that, in Europe, only the rich could afford. Canada was also far from communism, as the Hungarian refugees of 1956-57 could testify.

National Archives of Canada PA127043

Above: Hungarian immigrants attending after-hours schooling

German immigrants in Kitchener, Ontario

National Archives of Canada PA173822

farm and residential consumers, compared with 2.2 million in 1948 and 1.6 million in 1938).

Hydroelectricity was Canada's only major homegrown source of energy. The St. Lawrence and Ottawa River rapids, the falls at Niagara, and the great rivers of New Brunswick, Manitoba, and British Columbia all produced abundant energy — but not an unlimited supply. Demand and supply were not keeping pace, as brownouts in late 1940s' Ontario indicated. New dams were built in those years, too, but easily accessible new hydro sources were few and far between. The future, it appeared, would have to be thermal.

The second great source of energy was coal. Canadians consumed 40 million tons of it in 1949, 22 million imported from the United States and 18 million produced at home. Members of parliament from coal-mining districts in Nova Scotia and Alberta regularly complained that central Canada was not buying enough from them, while Ontario and Quebec industrialists replied that they needed the high-grade anthracite coal that domestic mines could not supply. As far as the national government was concerned, coal was both a source of internal political trouble and a constant drain on Canada's foreign exchange reserves. Nor was Ottawa entirely happy about Canada's dependence on American supply. The Americans were friendly neighbours, and naturally they wanted to sell as much coal as they could provide. But if there were a supply crisis, and the Cold War suggested there might be, would they look after Canada as well as they looked after themselves?

After coal, there was petroleum, oil, and gas. Canada had produced some of these resources as far back as the 1860s, but the supply was minute and the reserves — the amount of oil and gas estimated to remain in the ground — were getting steadily smaller. Ottawa and the rest of the country were therefore thrilled to learn in February 1947 that a well at Leduc, Alberta, outside Edmonton, had sent "a beautiful ring of black smoke floating skyward." Oil there was, and plenty of it.

The discovery brought immediate prosperity to north-central Alberta. Hotels and merchants could double their rates and triple their profits. Farmers could supply labour and local transport — $300,000 for one Leduc farmer in 1948, most of it considered to be capital gains and, under the tax laws of the day, virtually tax free. That year, sixty-eight new industries were established in Edmonton. "The city still looked like the drab market town that was the capital of a bankrupt Alberta in the 1930s," the journalist Blair Fraser wrote, but the city and the province were on their way to prosperity. Alberta's roads, the worst in Canada during the previous two decades, suddenly improved. Only the Alberta government, Social Credit (puritanical and clinging to its origins in the Depression) did not appear to change. It was, an astounded oilman with experience around the world exclaimed, "not only the most honest government, [but] the *only* honest government I've ever had to do with."

For Alberta, oil meant prosperity; for Canada, relief. The discovery, Ottawa officials hoped, would reduce Canada's dependence on American oil and gas and lessen the outflow of scarce American dollars. The dollar shortage was an embarrassment and a constraint. In November 1947 Canada signed on to a new international trading mechanism, the General Agreement on Tariffs and Trade, which aimed to reduce tariffs and trade barriers among the trading nations of the Western world. Yet the very day that the details of GATT were released to reporters in Ottawa, November 17, the government announced that it was imposing severe restrictions on imports of all kinds from the United States and availing itself of GATT provisions that protected troubled economies. During the winter of 1947-48 cabbage was the only green vegetable readily available in Canadian grocery stores.

Things quickly changed. Canada became a supplier and, especially, a vendor of Marshall Plan aid. Then the Leduc discovery seemed to be a signal for an inflow of investment, almost entirely from the United States. The oil patch had to be developed, and American oilmen and their families arrived, bringing with them millions of American dollars. In Ungava there was iron ore along the Quebec-Newfoundland border, and a market for it in Cleveland, Toledo, and Gary, the steelmaking cities of the American Midwest. The steel companies established the Iron Ore Company of Canada, with the mission of getting the ore to their smelters. To do it, they built a series of mines and a railway to move the ore to the port of Sept-Iles on the Gulf of St. Lawrence. The whole project cost in the hundreds of millions of dollars and, while it was building, the Canadian balance of payments improved. Around the mines and the port there appeared, instantly, modern housing with modern conveniences — a lesson for the people of the previously impoverished Quebec North Shore of the benefits of an American connection. Brian Mulroney, a teenager in the town of Baie-Comeau, took note.

Getting the ore to the upper Great Lakes posed another problem. Canals on the St. Lawrence from Montreal to Prescott were narrow and shallow, relics of the nineteenth century. For a generation the Canadian government had been struggling to improve the canals with a set of bigger waterways, to be called the St. Lawrence Seaway. But the St. Lawrence was an international waterway, shared with the United States, and competitive American railway interests kept Seaway issues bottled up in Congress. The iron ore project added considerably to the number of Seaway friends in Washington, and the Cold War subtracted from the fervour of its foes. Steel was a strategic material, after all, and the United States must continue to surpass the Soviet Union in steel production. Finally, at just the right moment, the Canadian government announced that it would build the Seaway itself. With the enthusiastic approval of President Harry Truman and the reluctant backing of his successor, Dwight D. Eisenhower, the American governmental structure swung into line. A treaty was signed, and money flowed from Washington to build American locks on the St. Lawrence.

The St. Lawrence Seaway and Power Project (for it included hydroelectric development along the St. Lawrence rapids) took five years to build, from 1954 to 1959. It opened with a flourish in June

A commemorative stamp showing the engineering design of the St. Lawrence Seaway.

1959, providing deep-water channel access from the ocean to the head of Lake Superior. The Seaway was another massive investment of the kind the St. Laurent government favoured. It came at a convenient time too, just at the end of a war in Korea.

The Korean War (the proverbial war in the wrong place at the wrong time) came to be regretted by virtually every country that engaged in it. Yet it had a profound effect on Canada and on Canadian society, and the effects lingered for decades. It gave content to the Cold War and set in concrete the divisions between East and West that, in the late 1940s, were already visible in Europe. The Cold War lost no time in spreading to Asia. There were well-established Communist parties in most Asian countries, but it was in China where communism enjoyed its most spectacular triumph. In 1949 Communist armies swept the corrupt and decadent Nationalist government of China into the sea and across the Taiwan Straits to a refuge on China's island province of Taiwan. China was weak, disorganized, and technologically backward, but the capture of the world's largest country — in terms of population — caught the imagination of other peoples struggling to be free.

Opposite: Canadian tank and soldier in the Korean War.

Communism, even in the late 1940s, seemed to promise equality, efficiency, and a quick fix of modernity in return for the sacrifice of the inefficient and heavily compromised system of bourgeois democracy — or so its enthusiasts and admirers believed. In August 1949 the Soviet Union exploded an atomic bomb, proof that communist science could equal the best the West could do. The communist leaders of 1949, Joseph Stalin of the Soviet Union and Mao Zedong of China, expected their ideology to triumph, and were not above extra assistance for those who wished to spread it faster. And so in the winter of 1949-50, Stalin and Mao agreed to supply the communist regime in North Korea with the equipment necessary to conquer its capitalist neighbour, South Korea. On June 25, 1950, North Korean tanks crossed the border and rolled south, with virtually nothing to oppose them.

Western governments were taken by surprise. Their response depended on the American government, and nobody expected the Americans to do anything much. External affairs minister Lester B. "Mike" Pearson had toured Asia in January 1950, passing through

National Archives of Canada PA128279

Tokyo, where he interviewed the senior American general and proconsul in Japan, Douglas MacArthur. MacArthur and his staff took the occasion to emphasize the "utter uselessness" of Korea to the West. "Pearson," a reporter wrote, "believed them." When the North Korean invasion occurred, Pearson wrote it off as a minor but regrettable incident.

The next day, however, President Truman announced that the United States would support South Korea by force of arms. Truman was not especially enamoured of Korea as a place to make war,

Courtesy of Department of National Defence

but he feared what the world would think if the United States abandoned even this small, weak country to communism. He had to consider, as well, Soviet possession of an atomic bomb, and how that might impress wavering governments. Truman therefore ordered a very reluctant General MacArthur to get himself and his army over to Korea, while he prepared to send reinforcements from the continental United States. Then Truman appealed to the United Nations to condemn and resist the North Korean aggression. Because the Soviet Union was boycotting UN meetings, the United States had its way, free of the Soviet veto.

Pearson and the Canadian government were astounded. Pearson was not displeased, since he cherished the hope that the United Nations, unlike the League of Nations in the 1930s, would become a true focal point of world public opinion. Perhaps, in the very long run, the United Nations might become an embryonic world government. For the moment, he recognized its usefulness in mobilizing world opinion — especially opinion in the "underdeveloped world," where poverty and desperation might seem to give an advantage to communism.

The Canadian cabinet reacted slowly. First the government sent three naval ships — a "token" contribution, an American diplomat sniffed. Surely three ships were more than a token, a Canadian counterpart protested. "All right," the American agreed. "Let's call it three tokens." Transport planes followed the ships. Finally, under American pressure and spurred on by Pearson, the cabinet agreed that Canada would send troops. Mackenzie King, who had a special dread of a war in Korea, might have objected. But King was dead: on the train returning from his funeral in Toronto at the end of July, the cabinet agreed that Canada would send troops to Korea. A special brigade was raised, to serve with a Commonwealth division in the United Nations Army in Korea.

Initially, victory crowned American arms. The North Korean Army was outflanked and sent reeling back over the border. American and South Korean troops followed. Next the Communist Chinese intervened, to prevent the awful possibility of a Communist government falling to capitalist arms, thereby encouraging a possible rebellion and resistance in China itself. The Chinese took the Americans by surprise, defeated them, and drove them south in December 1950. In Western capitals, including Ottawa, the news of defeat was badly received. Perhaps, the Canadian cabinet was told, Korea was a prelude to a communist attack in Europe in the spring. Canada must be ready. In response, the Canadian government more than doubled the size of Canada's armed forces and committed $5 billion to re-armament — about a quarter of the country's Gross National Product in 1950-51.

The NATO countries decided that they, too, must be ready. They created an allied supreme commander for Europe and appointed the American general and war hero Dwight D. Eisenhower to the posi-tion. Canada sent a reinforced army brigade and an air division

Canadian infantry on a Korean hillside.

Department of National Defence SF-4508

consisting of fighters to Europe in 1951. In one form or another, Canadian troops were to stay in Europe for the rest of the Cold War.

The war in Korea had, by the summer of 1951, turned into a stalemate, with the country divided more or less along the original boundary between North and South on the 38th parallel. Complicated negotiations for a truce followed: Washington learned, to its regret, that being leader of an allied coalition meant devoting a great deal of time and effort to the care and feeding of allies. Pearson in particular exasperated the Americans with his apparently insatiable appetite for compromise on what American diplomats and politicians took to be firm issues of principle. Finally, on July 27, 1953, an armistice was signed and the Korean War came to an inconclusive end, with neither side having achieved its preferred goals. In all, 309 Canadian soldiers died in Korea and 1200 were wounded.

The Korean War guaranteed that the single largest item in Canadian budgets for the next fifteen years would be defence and the military. Canada, which already had a small defence industry, built a bigger one. The relatively small Canadian aircraft industry received a shot in the arm. Canadair in Montreal built F-86 jets, an American design, while A.V. Roe in Toronto manufactured the CF-100, a jet interceptor, for the Royal Canadian Air Force. Soon A.V. Roe (also known as Avro) was designing a new all-weather supersonic jet interceptor, designated as the Arrow or CF-105. It would be Canada's passport into the next age of technology.

Defence production fell under the responsibility of C.D. Howe, the minister of defence production and of trade and commerce (dubbed "the minister of everything"). Howe was effectively the government's industry minister, its chief of economic planning. He kept the Canadian economy supplied with megaprojects, either private (Ungava iron ore) or public (rearmament and the St. Lawrence Seaway). Howe, with his experience in the war effort behind him, also worried about Canadian energy dependence on the United States.

Canada now had oil and gas in Alberta, but they were destined for markets in the United States, while American products brought by pipeline up the Mississippi Valley from Oklahoma, Louisiana, and Texas would supply eastern Canada. Howe planned instead for a pipeline across Canada, under Canadian control, to carry western oil and then western gas to Ontario and Quebec. Private enterprise duly constructed an oil pipeline, mostly in Canada but crossing American territory south of Lake Superior and supplying, en route, Midwest American markets.

For natural gas, Howe wanted an all-Canadian pipeline route. Ironically, to get it, he had to import American pipeline builders, and for the pipeline company (privately owned) to get finance, it had to go to New York. Finance was conditional on the American pipeline builders having control of the company. Worse still, from a political point of view, there was no money to build the pipeline through the sparsely settled region between Winnipeg and Sudbury. Howe would have to go to Parliament to get it.

For many years Howe had been accustomed to having his own way. He knew his limits, and did not seek to displace the prime minister or interfere in his colleagues' business. But he expected to prevail over the economy and the development of Canadian industry. Over the pipeline, he met some resistance. His project went back to the drawing boards several times, until, finally, in May 1956, it was ready. The governments of Canada and Ontario would finance an uneconomic length of pipe from Winnipeg to Sudbury. The pipeline company would initially be owned by Americans, but its shares would be made available to Canadians in the hope of achieving majority Canadian ownership. Howe insisted on a strict timetable, because he wanted to put pipe in the ground during the 1956 construction season. The government accordingly used the parliamentary device of closure to limit the time spent on debate right from the beginning.

Howe and his colleagues did not count on resistance from opposition parties, determined to exploit Howe's public image as an imperious old man (he was seventy-four and, in this case, was imperious). Debate in parliament focused on the denial of parliamentary and democratic rights rather than the pipeline policy or the energy issue. It focused as well on Howe's American origins and the presumption that, as an immigrant from the United States, he was still an American at heart. The political temperature rose, and with it anti-Americanism.

The government got its legislation passed in June 1956 after one of the wildest debates in Canadian history, but at great political cost

LABOUR, UNIONS, & STRIKES

National Archives of Canada PA163000

*T*he conservative Duplessis regime in Quebec was
notoriously unsympathetic to labour unions and,
especially, strikes. For labour organizers like Jean
Marchand (right), the strike against the Gaspé Copper
Company in 1957 was risky: violence was probable,
in this case less from the union than from management
or the police. Though Marchand and his colleagues
could not have predicted it, Quebec was on the verge
of a tremendous change, the Quiet Revolution. The
villains of the 1950s became the heroes of the 1960s
and 1970s, and Quebec became, for a time, almost a
labour-dominated society.

and damage to its self-image. Its opponents, especially the Progressive Conservatives, had a field day painting the Liberals as slavishly pro-American. Later that year circumstances handed the opposition another issue and another chance.

An international crisis erupted over the Suez Canal. Built in the 1870s, the Suez Canal was the link between Europe and the Orient and, in particular, between Great Britain and its empire in Asia. The British had owned it and guarded it since the 1880s, and for most of that time had also ruled Egypt, its host country, as a protectorate. But the British Empire was waning. In 1947 the British pulled out of India and Pakistan, and in 1948 out of Palestine. The very expensive British garrison around the Suez Canal was wound up in 1955, and Egypt acquired genuine independence for the first time in four centuries.

The 1955 deal brought a brief honeymoon in Anglo-Egyptian relations, but it did not last. When the British and Americans refused to lend money to Egypt in 1956, the Egyptians nationalized the Suez Canal, which was still owned by a private British firm. The British prime minister, Anthony Eden, was furious. If the Egyptians could push the British around, anyone could. To show that Great Britain was still a great power — though it really wasn't — Eden made a secret alliance with France and Israel to invade Egypt and seize the canal. Because he knew that the Canadians and Americans would not approve, he didn't tell them what he was planning to do.

But Canada and the United States were Great Britain's principal allies. Canada was especially closely linked because of its membership in the new British Commonwealth, the recent five-year sojourn of hundreds of thousands of Canadian soldiers in the British Isles during the Second World War, and heavy British immigration to Canada since 1945. (There were about 900,000 British-born living in Canada in 1951, out of 14 million persons, and 603,000 British immigrants arrived between 1945 and 1957.) There was a comfortable closeness between British and Canadian diplomats and politicians, partly because Great Britain really was no longer a great power and, consequently, appreciated Canadian assistance and the Canadian point of view.

Suez deeply divided Great Britain, as it divided Britain and Canada. Senior British civil servants regularly leaked information to their Canadian counterparts, expressing the hope that the Canadians could help get Britain out of the mess that Eden was creating. When the British, French, and Israelis actually attacked Egypt at the end of October 1956, the Canadians were horrified and the Americans, theoretically and actually the head of the Western alliance, were infuriated. Ex-colonial countries like India were also offended and, when the issue of Anglo-French aggression was brought up at the United Nations, as it was bound to be, it was obvious that Britain and France would be condemned by the UN majority and that the United States would do nothing to stop it.

Faced with economic troubles brought on by their invasion, the British and French collapsed. It was at this point that Canada intervened, using the failure of the Suez invasion as a means to create a United Nations peacekeeping force that would separate the combatants. Pearson, the prime mover of this idea at the United Nations (though he did not originate it) and, more than anyone else, responsible for its adoption, hoped to use the occasion to implant a permanent and supra-national UN presence in the troubled Middle East. On this point he was unsuccessful, but at least he got the peacekeepers in and the British and French out, with less humiliation than they might otherwise have received. In recognition of his achievement, Pearson was awarded the Nobel Peace Prize in December 1957 and, ever after, Canadians regarded peacekeeping with a proprietary affection. By the time he got the award, however, Pearson and the Liberals were out of office and a new government sat in Ottawa.

The St. Laurent Liberals called a general election for June 1957. They expected to win and they did not. Canadians remembered the Liberals' high-handed methods over the pipeline and they forgot, or did not understand, the purpose of a national energy policy. The Liberals had been in office a very long time. They had failed to solve problems or alleviate the grievances of large numbers of Canadians. Western wheat farmers were angered by American wheat giveaways that ate deeply into Canadian wheat sales. Yet the Americans ignored Canadian pleas to stop what was, in effect, a gigantic agricultural subsidy, and Canada could not afford to match it. The Liberals had given only a small increase in old age pensions. And so it went, grievance after grievance.

National Archives of Canada PA112695

For the first time in many years the principal opposition party, the Progressive Conservatives, had a lively and attractive leader, the veteran Saskatchewan politician and lawyer John Diefenbaker. Diefenbaker brought the Conservatives to a narrow victory over the Liberals — a minority government. He immediately enacted most of the goodies that the Liberals had refused, though he could, of course, do nothing about American wheat subsidies. Then, in the winter of 1958, he called a snap election against a new and inexperienced Liberal leader, Lester Pearson, and on March 31 he was rewarded with an overwhelming victory. Canadians had, as the Conservative slogan put it, chosen to "follow John." But where?

Davie Fulton raises John Diefenbaker's hand in a sign of victory; Donald Fleming applauds.

CHAPTER EIGHT

THE
STRANGEST
DECADE

Photographer Ken Bell, National Archives of Canada PA205843

*T*he 1960s should have been John Diefenbaker's decade. Instead, the Progressive Conservatives self-destructed and all the grey, safe underpinnings of Canadian life came unstuck. Teenagers grew rebellious and sported long hair. Casual sex became the norm as the birth control pill changed social mores. Popular music altered to the point where parents could scarcely bear to listen to it. Quebec grew restive and revolutionary. Governments completed the social welfare state, providing a cradle-to-grave security blanket for Canadians, but there seemed to be no stability in a world and nation come unglued.

None of these outcomes could be discerned when John Diefenbaker led the Progressive Conservative Party to the largest majority in Canadian history to that time. The Chief had seized on a gross tactical error by the new Liberal leader, Lester Pearson, in Parliament. The Diefenbaker minority government of 1957 had made a mess of the public's business, Pearson said, and it should hand power back to the Grits. Delighted, Diefenbaker called an election and steamrolled the opposition, leaving Pearson with only forty-nine seats and the Cooperative Commonwealth Federation in ruins. The Tories had 208 seats, with total control of every region, including Quebec, where they won two-thirds of the seats. The Diefenbaker era was under way.

It would not last long. Almost immediately, matters began to go awry. The great postwar economic boom was becoming frayed, unemployment was rising, and some Canadians were seriously concerned by the increasing American control over whole sectors of the economy. Labour unions wanted action to deal with jobs, and calls for wage increases did not abate. The government, which had campaigned on promises to deal with regional economic disparity, put up some money for the Maritimes, but the eastern Canadian economies continued to slip behind the rest. Diefenbaker had also called for the opening up of the North, but these speeches proved to be mainly rhetoric. The St. Lawrence Seaway, begun by the Liberal government, opened to traffic in 1959, giving access from the Atlantic Ocean to Lake Superior. The heart of the continent was now open to water-borne commerce, and cities like Toronto and Cleveland fancied themselves great world seaports. But the locks on the St. Lawrence River soon proved too small to handle the new and larger generation of ships that began to carry oil and containers around the globe.

Only in the West, his home region, did Diefenbaker deliver. His government proved remarkably effective in selling wheat to customers abroad, including China and the Soviet Union, and it created special funding programs for farmers. The West never forgot; it would remain loyal to the Chief when everyone else turned against him, and in Saskatchewan many — perhaps most — still think of him as Canada's greatest prime minister.

The wheat sales to the West's Cold War enemies drew mixed responses, not least in Washington. Indeed, Diefenbaker, whose speeches were always hawkish when he spoke about communism, came to be viewed as wobbly in the United States. Canada's defence budget strained as economic conditions worsened, and the army, navy, and air force all needed new equipment. Moreover, warfare seemed about to undergo dramatic change. In 1957 the Soviet Union launched *Sputnik*, the first satellite. The technology needed to put the satellite into orbit could also deliver an Intercontinental Ballistic Missile with a nuclear warhead to any point in North America.

This capability had a real impact on the government, which had inherited the Liberals' project to build a new fighter-interceptor for the Royal Canadian Air Force to use in the defence of North America. The Avro Arrow had the potential to be an effective weapons system, one able to deliver small nuclear-tipped missiles to blow Soviet bombers out of the sky. But the Arrow was very expensive, and no other country was interested in buying the Canadian-designed interceptor. The costs threatened to absorb the entire defence equipment budget, and the chiefs of staff and the defence minister became increasingly nervous. In 1959 the government screwed up its courage and cancelled the project. Avro promptly fired 14,000 workers, most in the Toronto area. That was bad enough, but Diefenbaker undertook in his announcement of the cancellation to accept Bomarc surface-to-air missiles from the United States to defend central Canada and the heartland of the United States from Soviet bombers. To be effective, the Bomarcs required nuclear weapons. Other defence decisions increased the reliance on "nukes": CF-104 fighter bombers stationed with NATO required nuclear weapons, the army was training for Honest John surface-to-surface missiles, and the navy wanted nuclear depth charges to counter Soviet submarines. The government never said no, and the re-equipment of the forces, except for the shot-down Arrow, went ahead. These defence issues would eventually bring down the government and the prime minister, but in 1959 there was scarcely a whisper of real protest against these decisions.

Curiously, after these major decisions on defence equipment that changed Canada's direction decisively, Diefenbaker earned a reputation for indecisiveness. His cabinet, for example, debated issues endlessly, including every execution of murderers. The number of cabinet and cabinet committee meetings escalated, to the despair of government officials. Strong personalities vied for the Chief's ear, pushing contradictory agendas that left the prime minister all but paralyzed. Worse, the economy continued to stagnate, and the finance minister, Donald Fleming, fell into deep disputes with the governor of the Bank of Canada, a fight that culminated in the sacking of the governor and a messy public spat.

Television had changed politics by the late 1950s. Finance Minister Donald Fleming, here with the Bank of Canada's James Coyne, tried hard to master the new medium, with indifferent success.

National Archives of Canada PA125785

National Archives of Canada C87201

An advocate of "funny money," the fiery populist and Créditiste leader Réal Caouette frightened the old parties in Quebec in the early 1960s. In 1962, Caouette held the balance of power in a minority House of Commons.

By 1962, with an election in the cards, the government was in trouble. The Liberals had remade themselves, the CCF had transformed itself into the New Democratic Party, and in Quebec populist Créditistes, led by the charismatic Réal Caouette, were making headway. The Chief was in low spirits, and the election result — a Conservative minority — left him depressed. A broken ankle kept him in pain, and a cabinet shuffle did nothing to relieve concerns about the leader's state of mind.

The threat of war soon compounded the problems. The Americans discovered that the Soviet Union had secretly installed nuclear missiles in Fidel Castro's Cuba, and nuclear war became a real prospect. When President Kennedy sent an envoy to Diefenbaker, with photographs of the Soviet installations, the Americans assumed that Canada would react in a supportive way. The prime minister and many in his cabinet were increasingly anti-American, and the decision to put the Canadian components of NORAD, the continent's air defence organization, on alert was delayed. The United States was furious, the military outraged, and Defence Minister Douglas Harkness ordered his aircraft to alert status on his own. In the greatest crisis since the end of the Second World War, Canada had been found wanting.

At the height of the crisis, with cabinet ministers and ordinary citizens believing that the world might end in a spasm of nuclear explosions, plans had been made for government in Canada to continue. A nationwide chain of bunkers, protected from blast and radiation, was built at the end of the 1950s. The largest, the national command centre, was at Carp, fifteen miles from Ottawa. Usually called "the Diefenbunker," this shelter was intended to hold some five hundred officials and service personnel in spartan surroundings. Radio and TV connected the bunker to the world outside, while special filters scrubbed the air clean of radiation. The prime minister's quarters were only marginally better than those of Private Jones, and there was no space for spouses. Fortunately, the bunker did not have to be used, and today it is a Cold War museum, a perfect example of what might have been.

The threat of annihilation frightened everyone. For the first time, protests against nuclear weapons began to grow. The Voice of Women called for nuclear disarmament, and Liberal leader Lester Pearson's wife, Maryon, joined up. The New Democratic Party was fervent in its opposition to "nukes," and the heat began to be felt in the Prime Minister's Office as thousands of letters called on Canada to opt out of the nuclear arms race.

After Cuba, Diefenbaker was receptive to this call. He had been badly bruised by American protests over his inaction during the crisis, and he believed that both he and Canada had been repeatedly snubbed and ignored by President Kennedy. In his cabinet, External Affairs Minister Howard Green, pushed by officials in his department, called for Canada to refuse to accept the nuclear weapons the government had agreed to a few years before. On the other side, Defence Minister Harkness believed that Canada had to meet its obligations and honour its commitments to its allies in NATO.

Nuclear weapons did in Diefenbaker's government. The Americans kept control of the weapons, but the Canadian government took the blame. "You get the bomb," President Kennedy tells Diefenbaker, "but we keep the matches."

VOUS L'ENTREPOSEZ.
VOUS NOUS GARDONS
LES ALLUMETTES.

CANADA

sans danger ?

National Archives of Canada C134520

The struggle tore the government apart, as Diefenbaker wavered between the two. The Kennedy government, frustrated at the lack of decision on nuclear weapons, precipitated the final crisis in January 1963 by issuing a denunciatory press release accusing the government, in effect, of incompetence, ineptitude, and prevarication. Within days, Harkness resigned, the government lost a confidence vote in the House of Commons, and more ministers jumped ship. The Tories were in ruins. In the election that followed, Diefenbaker fought against the United States government while Pearson's Liberals, now in favour of taking the nuclear warheads, campaigned for the country to go forward with its friends. The result, thanks to an extraordinary cross-country campaign by the prime minister, was a very narrow victory for the Liberals. Skilfully whipping up the

Arguably our greatest campaigner ever, Diefenbaker could be mesmerizing in stump speeches or when he met the people, as here in his Prince Albert constituency in 1968.

Photographer Frank Prazak, National Archives of Canada PA206638

latent anti-Americanism of Canadians, Diefenbaker's campaign had turned certain defeat into a nailbiter. "They" wanted him defeated — and they included Kennedy, the special interest groups, the East, and the cities. It was a superb effort at exploiting resentment — and it very nearly worked.

The winner and new prime minister, Lester Pearson, had led an effective opposition — after learning his political trade in the tough school of the House of Commons. Cheerful, engagingly disarming in one-on-one conversation, Pearson did not go over well in crowds or on television, where his slight lisp and jerky arm movements looked and sounded odd. His main difficulty was more serious, however, for Pearson did not want to be disliked and he tended to give all favour-seekers, all ministers wanting a policy pressed, the sense that he was on their side. Inevitably, claimants suffered disappointment, and accounts by disappointed ministers read devastatingly.

Pearson soon created a government chock full of former bureaucrats. He promised "Sixty Days of Decision" to announce new policy, and a restoration of order and efficiency. But matters fell apart very quickly. Finance Minister Walter Gordon's budget proposed curbs on U.S. investment and was torn to pieces by the financial media and by business. Diefenbaker provided an effective opposition in the House, and the Pearsonian flipflop on nuclear weapons continued to torment the anti-nuclear voices in the country. Suddenly Canada seemed to have become an uneasy place, difficult to govern.

Premier Jean Lesage and his troublesome minister René Levesque shaped Quebec's Quiet Revolution. For Ottawa, struggling to cope with French Canada's new demands, the revolution wasn't so quiet.

This was particularly true in Quebec. The Quiet Revolution had begun with the deaths of Maurice Duplessis and his successor, Paul Sauvé. Then the Liberals under former federal minister Jean Lesage won the 1960 provincial election on the cry of "Maîtres chez nous," or "Masters in our own house," and the pace of change accelerated daily. Education, hydro, an end to corruption — everything was open to modernization, everywhere was change. Surprisingly for the Pearson government, Lesage and his increasingly powerful minister René Lévesque, a former TV personality, proved difficult for the federal government to deal with, and relations between Ottawa and

National Archives of Canada PA163006

Quebec City became testy confrontations over every policy question. Pensions, for example, seemed a benign subject, but, in the new atmosphere, discussions over the creation of the Canada Pension Plan became a battle royal. Led by its cadre of effective bureaucrats, Quebec won, producing the superior Quebec Pension Plan, which worked with, but separate from, the Canada Pension Plan. That victory was a harbinger of what was to come. Pearson had reacted to the changed mood by creating the Royal Commission on Bilingualism and Biculturalism to study Quebec's place in Canada, but such efforts seemed insufficient at a time when many voices began calling for independence for Quebec. Some used bombs, others their votes, but unrest was everywhere. The promise of the 1960s had come unglued.

Separatist parties sprang up in Quebec, staging demonstrations and building support. Bilingualism and biculturalism were Ottawa's attempt to dampen tempers.

National Archives of Canada C5306

Pearson's government pressed on, the cabinet leaking like a sieve, with secrets and scandals spilling onto the top stories of the media. The prime minister had been Canada's greatest diplomat, but he did not seem effective as a leader. The voters sensed this failing, and although they had little love for the vicious tactics often used by Diefenbaker and his party, they denied Pearson a majority once more in the election of 1965. Even so, the Liberals' legislative record was superb. The CPP was one part of it, medicare another. Catastrophic illnesses could no longer bankrupt families, as the federal and provincial governments made medical insurance a cornerstone of Canadian life. By 1970 every province was aboard. Yet another element was Old Age Security. In effect, the Liberals completed the social welfare state begun by Mackenzie King.

State medicine was a swearword for many, especially doctors and insurance companies. Nonetheless, the developments in medicine made most diseases controllable. The polio epidemics of the 1940s and early 1950s, which always struck in the hot summer months when fearful families stayed away from the beach and avoided crowds, ended when an American doctor, Jonas Salk, discovered a vaccine against the paralyzing disease. In mass vaccinations in schools that roughly coincided with the rise of the Diefenbaker government, Canadian children received their shots. Polio disappeared as a threat, though its legacy of children in iron lungs and of thousands with wasted limbs remained.

The invention and wide distribution of the birth control pill might well have been the most significant event of the 1960s. With a simple pill taken daily, women could control their reproductive cycle. Sex without consequences — or at least sex without unwanted children — became available to anyone who wanted it in Canada. The resulting freedom — to some it was licence — changed the way Canadians behaved. Birth rates began to fall through the 1960s as parents planned their families, spacing children to suit their convenience. As journalist John Fraser wrote, "It wasn't until the formal papal ban on birth control that many Newfoundland Catholics in the more remote outports even knew the pill existed. Inquiries into where to get it began the moment the mass was over; the same may have occurred in Quebec." Exactly. In Quebec, where the pill coincided with the Quiet Revolution and the weakening influence of the Roman Catholic Church,

The 1960s were hip, a time for swingers, for sexual experimentation, for new music and new style.

the birth rate went from the highest in Canada to the lowest in what seemed the blink of an eye. For the young, the pill opened up a sexual wonderland that fed the rebelliousness and revolt of the 1960s. The world of young male-female relationships went from dating and tea dances to sexual intercourse, fellatio, cunnilingus, marijuana, and freedom. Casual sex was a form of protest for many, a reaction against the square, straight 1950s, and in the 1960s the world changed.

Hair styles altered, too, mostly for men. The 1940s and 1950s were the era of short hair and brush cuts, and if a moustache was worn, it was a small brush under the nose or, in the military, a handlebar. But in the 1960s "hair, glorious hair" suddenly grew. Boys looked like Renaissance courtiers, long hair curling down their backs. For many, a ponytail was de rigueur; for others, beards or sideburns of amazing variety became the norm. Blacks favoured the afro. The hair revolution happened so quickly that, by the end of the decade, anyone with a brush cut could almost be guaranteed to be in the military or the police.

National Library of Canada, Music Division, Vancouver Symphony Orchestra Program, Jan. 1966

THE SIXTIES

Photographer F. Ross, *Toronto Star*

Photographer Frank Prazak,
National Archives of Canada 206655

Courtesy Judith Hanna

The very word conveyed a sense of change, and Toronto's Yorkville area was the centre of the action. Clubs, coffee houses, drugs, loud new music, boys with long hair, and a sudden sexual freedom created by the availability of the birth control pill all combined to create a special time and place. Older Canadians were not amused, seeing old values crumbling before their eyes. There were police confrontations with young protesters and Toronto's City Council tried its best to shut down Yorkville. It failed, just as the city fathers did in Vancouver, Montreal, and every city in North America.

good posture and dressing properly. Automobiles guzzled gas prodigiously as they hauled tons of metal along the roads; Japanese cars were not even a dream. And culture began to develop. The creation of the Canada Council spurred a boom in the arts, and touring companies took dance and theatre virtually everywhere.

Photographer Frank Prazak, National Archives of Canada PA206646

Photographer Ken Bell, National Archives of Canada PA206

Music changed too. The 1950s had seen teenagers dancing to groups such as The Four Lads and The Crewcuts, blandly harmonic. Then Elvis came on the scene, with a new sound. Presley's first visit to Canada came in 1957, and the hip-swinging, frank sexuality of his appearance and sound heralded a new era. Kids went wild. In Toronto, 25,000 youth jammed Maple Leaf Gardens. In Ottawa, Presley denied that he was vulgar, as the Separate School Board had charged. "You have to put on a show for the people," he protested. "You can't just stand there like a statue." Had the young lost their morals? Presley was asked. "No, they haven't. You're not going to stop a group of young people from having a nice time, because they only grow up once and they're gonna have a ball." In Vancouver they did, with 25,000 screaming fans storming the stage and overrunning the police. Only the Presley national anthem, "You Ain't Nothing But a Hound Dog," restored order. Parents shook their heads, but Presley was tame by comparison with the boisterous, foul-mouthed entertainers who dominated the 1960s. The Beatles, however, were neither foul-mouthed nor especially boisterous, and they would become the enduring musical influence of the decade.

At home, times were good. Every house had a television set, and aerials sprouted atop them all. The middle class put broadloom on the floors and wallpaper on the walls. Few houses had any original art, as most sported wedding photos and pictures of the kids. "Hi-fis" — record players with better sound — appeared in the late 1950s, but soon gave way to "stereos" — two speakers with distinct sound. Watching television news became a danger to people's mental health. Quicker air travel meant that news footage could be taken one day and broadcast at supper time the next. The war in Vietnam, pitting the United States and South Vietnam against the North Vietnamese and guerillas in the South, was on the news every day, with graphic combat footage available in North Americans' living rooms. This coverage was very different from the censored newsreels that Canadians had watched during the Second World War and Korea. No one had seen anything like this before; no one had watched maiming and death inflicted by and on American soldiers in a war that was notably brutal. Very soon, protest arrived over the border, carried by young Americans fleeing the draft or deserting from the U.S. forces.

There are no firm figures on the number of Americans who came to Canada to escape military service, but it may be as many as one hundred thousand. Most were college age, and many were already well educated. All had decided to leave their homeland for the sometimes strange Canada. They made friends quickly and influenced young Canadians, many of whom had already decided that their elders were hypocritically supporting the U.S. war machine while tut-tutting at the bombing of North Vietnam. University teach-ins, marches, denunciations of American-owned companies that made weaponry, and attacks on the Pearson government for its supposed moral cowardice became almost daily occurrences, peaking whenever events in Vietnam took a dramatic turn. Amazingly, the Canadian government did not try to close the border to "dodgers," even though polls indicated that the Americans' war had widespread support in Canada into the 1970s.

The arrival of the young Americans coincided with the burgeoning of Canadian universities. By the 1950s most people assumed that high-school education was a right; by the end of the 1960s, university was almost a right. From being the post-secondary destination of a few, universities became the place of the many. The old institutions — Dalhousie, Laval, McGill, Queen's, Toronto, Western, Manitoba, Saskatchewan, Alberta, and British Columbia — simply could not handle the numbers and new universities popped up in wheat fields. York, Simon Fraser, Regina, Lethbridge, Brandon, Lakehead, UQAM — there seemed no end to the new institutions or to the religious colleges that scrambled to get public moneys by going nondenominational. It was a stunning change, not least in Quebec, where the Church's hold on learning disappeared. L'Université de Québec à Montréal effectively symbolized the change by having its main building rise out of the façade of a former church.

It was impossible to staff these new schools without importing professors. There were too few Canadians with PhDs, and recruiting teams that formerly went to Britain for Oxbridge dons now visited the American Historical Association and the Modern Language Association. A flood of Americans came north, many trying to escape the impact of the Vietnam War, others looking for a new start, and most intending not to remain for long. Many of these new hires were radical in politics, and their impact on students was strong. Concern developed that this huge number of American professors was erasing Canada's literature, history, and sociology under the weight of "foreign" ideas. By the 1970s there was a push for "Canadianization," for Canadian content, and for citizenship tests for academics.

Nationalism dominated the 1960s. Pearson's government gave Canada its own anthem and flag, the latter after a bitter debate marked by blatant anti-Quebec racism from Conservatives. Concerns over the increasing U.S. control of the economy filled debates within and without the government, with Finance Minister Walter Gordon the leader of the economic nationalist position. Gordon made some headway, but the continentalist wing of the Liberal Party was, if anything, stronger and had the prime minister's ear, especially after the minister's resignation in 1965. There was little in the way of legislation to slow continental integration; indeed, in the area of defence, the Pearson government moved even closer to the United States.

The highlight of the nationalist fervour came in 1967, the centennial of Confederation. Every town and city had its projects, arenas

Expo 67 was Canada's showcase to the world in Centennial year. No longer was it good, grey Canada. Now Montreal was the modern, bilingual city, the heart of a vibrant nation. Or so Canadians said and hoped.

National Archives of Canada C18536

sprang up across the land, and culture went on the road to small towns and large cities alike. The Canada Council, founded in 1957, was paying off in a big way, as writers like Robertson Davies and Mordecai Richler, painters like Jack Bush, pianists like Glenn Gould, and arts companies like the Royal Winnipeg Ballet and the Montreal Symphony Orchestra became known across the country. Subsidized books on every subject also carried the Centennial logo. At the same time, a train with historical exhibits travelled from coast to coast. The highlight of the celebratory year, however, was the world's fair created at vast cost on islands off Montreal. Expo 67 was a wondrous show, bringing the world to Canada's greatest city in ways that amazed and delighted millions of visitors.

President de Gaulle, greeted by ecstatic crowds in Quebec, gave separatism credibility with his meddling in Canada's affairs. The federal government promptly ordered him out of Canada.

There was one fly in the ointment. When he came to Canada for a state visit and a tour of Expo, President Charles de Gaulle of France seized the opportunity to make mischief. Quebec separatism had been sport for intellectuals and a few Marxist terrorists playing at turning *la belle province* into Algeria, but de Gaulle

Courtesy of J.L. Granatstein

brought it into the mainstream. In an address from Montreal City Hall, he delivered his text and then segued into a series of *vives*, his last being "Vive le Québec libre." The audience went wild, but in Ottawa the government was stunned at the French leader's support for separatism. Prime Minister Pearson bluntly ordered the wartime leader of Free France out of the country, reminding the world that Canada was free and, moreover, that a hundred thousand Canadians had died in two wars to keep France free. English Canadians cheered Pearson's riposte, but countless Québécois felt a secret joy in de Gaulle's blatant tweaking of the Anglo nose. Separatism now was *the* issue.

This new challenge mattered because the septuagenarian Pearson was in his final months as prime minister. He had led the Grits to two minority governments in a row, and, although his legislative record was impressive, there was a widespread sense that it was time for new blood. The Conservatives had "dumped Dief" in a bloody convention in 1967, replacing him with Nova Scotia premier Robert Stanfield, a cautious, careful, slow-speaking man. The Liberal contenders, too, seemed cut from similar cloth. Foreign Minister Paul Martin was an old pro, former minister Robert Winters was smooth as silk and very pro-business, and other possible candidates failed to inspire.

But there was Justice Minister Pierre Elliott Trudeau, a forty-eight-year-old swinging bachelor from Montreal who had come into Parliament only in 1965. Intelligent, tough, a man with a reputation as an adventurer and public intellectual, Trudeau first came to wide public notice at a federal-provincial conference in early 1968 when he savaged Quebec's Union National premier Daniel Johnson in a televised debate on constitutional change. He also reformed Canada's outdated Criminal Code, including archaic laws on sex. "The state has no place in the bedrooms of the nation," Trudeau famously said. Those who were looking for a new kind of leader became interested. Those who wanted a tough federalist who could take on the rising separatist tide in Quebec had also found their man.

New ideas seemed needed by 1968, and in Pierre Trudeau, here flanked by Quebec Premier Daniel Johnson and Prime Minister Pearson, French and English Canadians found their leader. Young, vigorous, intelligent, Trudeau was a Quebec federalist whose vision would dominate the rest of the century.

Photographer Duncan Cameron, National Archives of Canada PA117460

CHAPTER NINE

A DISAPPOINTING DECADE

Illustration by David Annesley, by permission of *Exile Editions*

If the late 1960s was the season of youth, the 1970s was the decade of the baby boom. In 1968 Pierre Elliott Trudeau came to power, bringing a new generation in his train. Thousands of boomers cast their first votes that year and they cast them, by and large, for Trudeau. The new prime minister swept to power on the strength of an attitude and a personality (his) and if baby boomers appreciated anything it was attitude. Trudeau was fond of quoting a French maxim, "Style expresses the man himself." It was the way things were done that would be different.

The Trudeau era began with a search for a French Canadian to succeed Lester Pearson as prime minister. Pearson believed (with good reason) that French Canadians were doubtful of their place in Canada. A lively separatist movement had emerged in Quebec and, in 1967, had captured a prominent and charismatic provincial politician, René Lévesque, to lead it.

Trudeau, a law professor and public intellectual from Montreal, had joined the Pearson cabinet only in 1967, though in the senior position of minister of justice. He had a passionate commitment to federalism, and an equally passionate antagonism to Quebec nationalism, which he considered narrow-minded and reactionary. A considerable if controversial figure in Quebec, Trudeau turned out to have qualities that appealed in English Canada as well. He had style. Though forty-eight years of age, he dressed and acted like someone twenty years his junior. Rich, nonchalant, elegant, Trudeau personified what the baby boomers would like to be. A foe of outdated conventions, wearing ascots to Parliament and sandals in public, the minister of justice signalled that life with Pierre would be very different from life with Lester. Younger Canadians could hardly wait.

In April 1968 Trudeau narrowly won the Liberal leadership at a convention in Ottawa and promptly went on to party with his youthful supporters. Two weeks later he was prime minister, and he called a general election for June 25. The election campaign that followed — two months of it — met the 1960s' definition of a "love-in." Younger Canadians, especially younger female Canadians, were aware that Trudeau was a bachelor, Canada's most eligible, and they mobbed him at campaign stops wherever he went.

Opposite: Pierre Trudeau gave Canadians something they had never before had — a leader they could admire for his appearance as well as his mind. Trudeau oozed charisma and voters either loved him or despised him. There was no middle ground. But all came to agree over his almost sixteen years in office that he remade Canada.

The day before the election was St.-Jean Baptiste Day in Quebec and, as an honoured French Canadian, Trudeau sat on the reviewing stand for the parade. It proved to be the most eventful St.-Jean Baptiste Day parade in history, since Trudeau's separatist opponents decided to disrupt proceedings with a shower of garbage and bottles. Most of the dignitaries on the reviewing stand quickly retreated, but the cameras caught Trudeau defying missiles and rioters, standing his ground as the parade dissolved into chaos around him. Under the velvet exterior of the trendy politician there lurked a steely determination. On Quebec, Canadians could see, there would be no compromise.

The next day Trudeau received a thumping majority in the House of Commons, including most of the seats in Quebec. For the next eleven years, until June 1979, he would be prime minister, the longest term since Mackenzie King (and he would add four more years in the 1980s). Yet his longest single term, spanning the 1970s, was a disappointment. Given the high hopes of his supporters, the enthusiasm of his first election, the mobilization of youth, the promise of openness ("participatory democracy" was the phrase) disappointment may have been inevitable. But by 1979, to borrow another phrase from the period, "it seemed like nothing happened." How could this be?

Youth and the youth culture were everywhere. Given the number of Canadians under thirty (13.75 million out of 21.5 million in the 1971 census) it could hardly be otherwise. Most Canadians were young, and, moreover, they could afford to be young. Canadians in the 1970s were better off than they ever had been before — matching Americans, in terms of average incomes, for the only time in Canadian history. Between 1965 and 1975 average Canadian incomes rose 55 percent, compared with 16 percent in the United States. In 1976, statisticians reported, the median Canadian family pulled in just over $15,000, while its median American counterpart made just under.

These were impressive figures. The money was there for self-expression, and Canadians did not hesitate to spend. Small wonder that the 1970s became a decade of vivid colours and exaggerated styles. It was a time of experimentation in clothing. Men's clothes since 1900 had varied only in shades of grey, black, or brown, and in fabric from tweed to worsted. Only the size of lapels and the width of pant leg could reveal which decade you were in. But at the end of the 1960s bell-bottom trousers, previously confined to the navy, entered male fashion. Ties expanded as their usage shrank. Men adopted turtleneck sweaters and hung medallions on the front. Mao and Nehru jackets proclaimed solidarity with the Third World — a

Trudeau in China: Communist functionaries wearing Mao suits receive Prime Minister Trudeau. At home, Mao suits were what the well-dressed radical craved.

Photographer Duncan Cameron, National Archives of Canada PA136978

new term, just becoming fashionable. Everywhere there were blue jeans, carefully washed and pounded to look suitably worn. New fabrics, double-knit and polyester, appeared on men and women alike.

The revolution in women's clothing was equally startling. The most obvious trend was shorter, much shorter, skirts, starting around 1965. The skirts could go up because underneath them was another invention of the 1960s, pantyhose, which were virtually universal among younger women by 1968. Women, more than men, could flaunt the fashionable colours of the 1970s — especially orange. The Trudeau Liberal leadership campaign in 1968 adopted orange for the mini-dresses of its female staff and its muted but chic signage.

For the athletic (and eventually for the merely sloppy) there were jogging suits. For a brief moment, polyester leisure suits were fashionable and, because of their general comfort and ease of care, they outlasted fashion by many years, coming to denote indifference to fashionable trends. There was also a brief flare for footwear called earth shoes, until podiatrists protested that these ecological items were actually ruining wearers' feet. Finally, later in the 1970s, there were platform shoes for women and men, popularized in the disco movie *Saturday Night Fever*.

In all these things Canada followed international, particularly American, styles. So close to the United States, so outnumbered by Americans, some Canadians felt uneasy. Would Canada survive if Canada, its lifestyle, culture, and economy, were indistinguishable from the American? Were Canadians, after all, what a waspish American ambassador called "second-rate Americans"?

Canadians in the 1970s thought not. The United States was mired in a war in far-off Vietnam, to which it sent regular drafts of young conscripts. American cities erupted in race riots (Los Angeles, Detroit, Washington). Nervous diplomats watched from the roof of the Canadian Embassy in the American capital as the police sirens and the rioters drew uncomfortably close. American politics did not absorb youth, as in Trudeau's Canada. Instead, alienated youth spoke out against the core values of the country. The war in Vietnam was finally lost, and the United States absorbed its first clear defeat in war. Even in America, it seemed as if the great republic had lost its way.

Younger Canadians tended to adopt the views of the alienated fraction of younger Americans. The United States and its society and economy had taken a wrong turn, symbolized by the Vietnam War. Canada, by contrast, was touted as a "peaceable kingdom." Draft dodgers crossed the border, making the fringes of Canada's larger universities a virtual American suburb. What the Americans found was a society that was indeed quieter than the one they had left behind. There was no war and no draft. Canadians were a bit stodgy, some reported, but the cities were clean and safe. Except for the fact that they could not actually go home, the draft dodgers found Canada pleasingly comfortable. The food, the smells, the clothes were, after all, indistinguishable from what they had known before. So were the sounds, except in Quebec.

The Canadian government knew this was so. Canadian sounds were, in fact, American sounds. Canadian radio stations played American or, at any rate, international music, given that the British group the Beatles were the musical icons of the decade. This domination produced occasionally bizarre effects. The Windsor radio station CKLW, playing American rock, dominated the Detroit airwaves and was a major influence on what kind of music was played in and around the U.S. Midwest. But rock had its Canadian branch, and so did folk and the other musical fashions of the 1970s. Gordon Lightfoot, Joni Mitchell, and Neil Young were all playing in Toronto coffeehouses and nightclubs. The American musician Rompin' Ronnie Hawkins made Toronto his home and spawned a generation of disciples, "The Band" being the most notable. When the government decreed that Canadian radio stations must play a certain amount of "Canadian content," the notion did not appear to be as strange or as ludicrous as it once had been. The Canadian quota became a part of Canadian life, a sign that the government was anxiously watching the border.

The ultimate symbol of Americanization, however, was economic. A large part of Canadian industry was American owned. Many Canadians liked it that way. American investment in Canada brought jobs and modernization. In Alberta, American oil companies, and in Ontario, American automobile companies, dominated the industrial landscape. Canadian governments encouraged the investment: American, Canadian, British, or Swedish (if it produced jobs it was good). As a result, a relatively high proportion of the Canadian economy was owned elsewhere. Pundits totted up the figures and worried. Petroleum, other mining and smelting, and manufacturing in general were all more than 50 percent foreign controlled, according to government statistics. Critics duly denounced the statistics and attributed the prevalence of foreign ownership and control of Canadian industries to a spineless government. Promoters of foreign investment, especially outside prosperous Ontario, condemned the critics as people who would slay the goose that laid the golden eggs of economic diversification. The Trudeau government

The Medium is the Message

*O*utside Canada, the English professor and philosopher Marshall McLuhan was better known even than the prime minister, Pierre Trudeau. McLuhan's theories about communications caught the imagination of the world: the medium, he intoned, was the message. McLuhan himself almost became part of the medium, a celebrity in a country where celebrities were few and far between. He could appear and be recognized in a Woody Allen movie *Annie Hall* as a kind of cultural icon on the block. In this photo, McLuhan is framed by print — the first "medium" he had examined.

Photographer Louis Forsdale, National Archives of Canada PA172802

duly commissioned studies that confirmed what everybody — in Ottawa and Toronto anyway — believed: foreign investment was a problem and Ottawa must do something about it.

In 1971 the government created a Crown agency, the Canada Development Corporation, to intervene in the market and promote Canadian ownership. The result, by the end of the decade, was a rash of government-owned companies, notably aircraft manufacturers. It kept high-tech jobs in Canada, but at a cost. There was also a Foreign Investment Review Agency, established in 1974, to screen foreign takeovers and make sure they were in the public interest. The agency in fact approved most foreign investment, but it slowed it down, and often made it subject to strict conditions that irritated investors and annoyed foreign governments.

The government also embarked on an ambitious program of taking jobs to workers, instead of moving workers to jobs. This program aimed to ensure that people in places like Cape Breton Island, far from Canada's industrial centre and handicapped by obsolete industries, had a chance to stay put and still earn a decent living. Billions of dollars were poured into everything from steel to sheep farming, but the result always seemed to be demands for more money. Soon the Canadian government was involved in propping up a wide variety of industries from coast to coast.

It cannot be said that the Trudeau government believed in hasty action. Its initiatives, though often ill digested, enjoyed a surfeit of process. Circumstances that seemed to demand one kind of response sometimes changed completely before the government had made up its mind what to do. The best example of prolonged policy was the question of what to do with Canada's oil and gas industry. Before 1968, Canadian policy on petroleum was relatively simple: the government encouraged a high-cost Canadian petroleum industry, located mostly in Alberta, by requiring people in the West and Ontario to buy its products. Meanwhile, consumers in Quebec and the Atlantic provinces could buy cheaper overseas oil off the ship, so to speak. After all, the Atlantic and Quebec regions were less prosperous than Ontario, and Quebec's political allegiance was shaky. Why provoke voters with expensive Canadian products when cheaper oil from abroad was readily available? The Middle

East and Venezuela produced plentiful supplies of oil, with apparently unlimited prospects of producing more. Meanwhile, since Canada too produced oil in abundance, the Canadian government tried to open American markets for Canadian exports.

In the early 1970s this situation changed. Oil no longer seemed to be in unlimited supply, and Western consumers were insatiable. Big cars travelled at high speeds over an ever-expanding highway network in Canada and the United States. Ships and planes as well as automobiles used gasoline, and buildings were almost entirely heated by oil or natural gas. Coal (dark, smoky, bulky, and old-fashioned, but definitely produced in abundance in North America) was on the way out. The same was true, with variations, in the United States and in Western Europe. Suddenly, around 1960 in the United States and around 1970 in Canada, the oil companies reported an ominous development: their geologists were no longer discovering vast new fields of oil and gas. Could an oil shortage be in prospect?

This news was music to the ears of oil producers. If supply was limited, prices could finally rise. In the early 1970s overseas oil-producing countries, led by Saudi Arabia and Venezuela, decided to overturn the terms of trade. They had sold cheap; now they would sell dear. Western consumers, they reasoned, would not be able to find substitutes, either different producers of oil and gas or alternative energy sources like nuclear energy. Canadians, who had focused on whether American companies owned too many Canadian oil wells, were unprepared for a sudden rise in the price of overseas oil in the fall of 1973. Oil prices, measured in dollars per barrel, doubled and then tripled. Between 1972 and 1979 they rose from $2.70 to more than $30 a barrel. An oil boycott of Western countries by Arab oil suppliers increased the sense of uncertainty. Suddenly the Alberta oil reserves looked considerably more attractive to consumers in Quebec and the Atlantic region.

The Trudeau government was doubly unprepared for this development. It had called a general election for October 1972 and had almost lost. With its existence hanging by the thread of a couple of opposition votes in the House of Commons, the government had to do what was politically expedient. It announced it would extend oil and gas pipelines from Montreal down the St. Lawrence.

It would guarantee security of supply — security of Canadian supply — to Quebec consumers. Canadian oil was suddenly a political advantage in Quebec. It would tax oil exports and use the revenue to subsidize Atlantic consumers. It announced the formation of a government-owned oil company, Petro-Canada, and bought up the interests of a Belgian-owned firm to do it. In the final analysis, to meet the oil shortage and supply Canadians the government would unbalance the national budget, and it did. From 1974 on, the Canadian government ran budget deficits.

In the short term, deficits were a secondary consideration, behind the government's political survival. In this respect, the government was very successful. Outmanoeuvring the opposition parties, Trudeau forced an election in July 1974 and was rewarded with a majority in the House of Commons. Obviously, expediency paid dividends.

Yet the second Trudeau majority government proved as frustrating as its predecessor had. The basic problem was that people expected it to solve a long list of problems, while the government did not know how to solve them. Inflation was a problem (12 percent at the beginning of 1975) so in October the government tried to freeze prices and incomes. Inflation did fall, temporarily, but by 1977 it was back to 10 percent.

In the 1960s Expo 67 had fuelled Canada's sense of optimistic progress. The chosen symbol for the 1970s was the 1976 Olympics, also in Montreal. Yet almost everything about the Olympics went wrong. Montreal's perennial mayor, Jean Drapeau, won the games for his city and took charge of the planning. Everything would be on the grand scale. Montreal, which was languishing economically

The Montreal Olympics of 1976 were only partly successful, and financially disastrous for the city.

behind its rival Toronto, needed a boost, in morale and in money. Drapeau planned for an Olympic stadium that went beyond mere practicality, though it would permanently house Montreal's baseball team, the Expos. Unluckily for Drapeau, the city's construction unions saw a heaven-sent opportunity to make money, recently scarce in the city's depressed economy. A long series of strikes and delays pushed costs ever upwards. Drapeau reassured citizens, saying that his Olympics could no more have a deficit than a man could have a baby. By the time the stadium costs hit $1 billion, observers were checking the mayor for signs of pregnancy.

The "Big O" (oval as well as Olympic) was certainly big — 60,000 seats — as well as costly. A gracefully arcing tower, delicately birdlike in a distant perspective, suspended a retractable roof over the stadium. The roof was actually a fabric that could be pulled up or lowered according to the weather outside. Given Montreal's winters, it doubled the time the stadium could be used; if it didn't work, however, the stadium's economics would suffer. Regrettably it did not work. At first, delays were ascribed to fine-tuning, the inevitable consequence of such a daring design. But as delay followed delay, it became clear that more than fine-tuning was needed. What was really needed was money, and lots of it. The retractable roof was finally ready for use in 1987, eleven years behind target. But the fabric tore, the retraction cycle had problems, and authorities decided to keep the stadium roof permanently closed. But that did not end fabric tears, and by the 1990s parts of the building were falling down too. At tax time Montreal and Quebec residents had reason to remember Drapeau and to damn the "edifice complex" that had led the city onto an architectural path of folly.

The Big O largely completed Montreal's skyline. Building projects were few and far between in the later 1960s and 1970s as the old metropolis steadily lost ground economically to Toronto. The Ontario capital, in contrast, was booming. Especially galling was the fact that Montreal's two premier banks, the Royal Bank of Canada and the Bank of Montreal, decided to base their head offices in Toronto and built tower complexes to house them. Canada's biggest department store, Eaton's, built the country's most spectacular atrium, the Eaton Centre, in Toronto. At the same time, Eaton's abandoned its money-

Photographer Frank Prazak, National Archives of Canada PA206664

losing catalogue business, which had given the store a presence across Canada since the late nineteenth century. Canada, along with its commercial symbols, was not quite what it had been.

The country was changing in other ways too. The birth rate, in decline since the mid-1960s, continued to fall. So did the death rate, while immigration remained at respectable levels. The Canadian population therefore increased, though more slowly than in the 1950s or 1960s. The number of children, however, declined, with the result that Canada's age profile by the end of the decade was perceptibly greyer than it had been in 1971. The age of youth was coming to an end.

The 1970s saw a marked change in the internal distribution of the Canadian population. From the 1930s to the 1970s, Canadians and immigrants had tended to move west or to Ontario. Quebec grew, thanks to its high birth rate, and, within Quebec, Montreal remained a magnet because of its assemblage of service industries and its high-tech aviation, electronic, and pharmaceutical sectors. In the 1970s this pattern changed. English Canadians were often uninformed about developments and prospects inside Quebec, and especially inside the province's French-language majority. When the birth control pill hit Canada in the early 1960s, some observers believed that Quebec, because of its Catholic majority and the dominant role played by the Roman Catholic Church, would remain immune. That did not prove to be the case. The Catholic Church crumbled in the face of a secularizing trend. Church attendance plummeted and the number of clergy shrank. Older priests had to handle smaller congregations. The church sold off old buildings, in some cases to serve as bingo halls. Visitors to Quebec noticed the difference.

The difference meant that, in some senses, Quebec was becoming more like the rest of Canada, where the secularizing trend was a little older and more widespread. Younger Quebeckers did not see the Catholic Church as the only obsolete institution they wanted to get rid of. Just as the church had enforced submission and conformity in the social and intellectual sphere, so the economy and the state had forced French-speaking Quebeckers into the service of an English-language business and political establishment. Now, at the end of the 1960s, a new book, *White Niggers of North America*, caused excitement in Quebec universities.

Even more excitement was caused by a continuing terrorist campaign against the Canadian government and the institutions of the English-speaking elite. Protesters demanded that McGill University in Montreal be transformed into a French-language school. During a police strike in 1970, rioters trashed the windows of downtown English-language department stores. A bomb wrecked the interior of the Montreal stock exchange. Then, at the beginning of October 1970, terrorists kidnapped the British trade representative from his home in Montreal. In return for his release, they demanded immunity, money, the release of other terrorists from jail, and a flight to Cuba. When the authorities resisted and delayed, other terrorists kidnapped Quebec's minister of labour, Pierre Laporte.

The result was a full-scale crisis. A pro-federalist Liberal government had recently been elected in Quebec, headed by the youthful Robert Bourassa. In Ottawa, Trudeau kept a close eye on the political situation in Quebec City, but it was not hard to see that Bourassa and his advisers were close to panic. Ministers flew their families out of the province, while self-appointed mediators contemplated the possibility of a government of "national" unity — one that would comprise separatists as well as federalists in an attempt to bridge the political chasm. Given that the province had a government that had been democratically elected six months before, this solution would have changed not only the political landscape but the rules of the political game.

The October Crisis of 1970: soldiers and roadblocks in Montreal.

Photographer Frank Prazak, National Archives of Canada PA206660

Bourassa opted for the game that he knew. He first asked Trudeau to send in the army, which he did, and then to proclaim a state of emergency and invoke Canada's emergency legislation, the War Measures Act. Trudeau obliged, proclaiming a state of "apprehended

Photographer Frank Prazak, National Archives of Canada PA206659

The October Crisis: soldier guarding a police station.

insurrection" and giving the police special powers to arrest and detain suspected terrorists and their sympathizers. Public opinion, across Canada as well as in Quebec, was almost unanimous in support of the government's action. Pro-terrorist demonstrations subsided in Montreal. The army met no impediment to its operations, either in Quebec or in Ottawa, where soldiers were much in evidence guarding politicians. Indignant reporters quizzed Trudeau: how far would he go, they asked in a confrontation on the steps of the Parliament Buildings. "Just watch me," Trudeau replied. It was "more important to preserve law and order" in society, he said, than to gratify the desires of "bleeding hearts" who could not see the necessity for a display of force.

The police and the soldiers operated slowly. They were not in time to save the unfortunate labour minister, who was murdered by his captors, but in early December they located the British diplomat and negotiated his freedom in return for a free trip to Cuba for his kidnappers. The murderers were discovered hiding in a country basement. They were tried and convicted and, after serving jail terms, released. The army was withdrawn, and the government's emergency powers eventually lapsed. Most of the supposed terrorists arrested were simply released; apart from the real kidnappers and murderers, none was convicted.

This October Crisis was one of the most dramatic events in Canadian history. In many respects it was reassuring. It showed that the number of terrorists in Quebec was, in fact, quite small. It

PEACEKEEPERS

Department of National Defence, ISC 84-351

Department of National Defence, ISC 84-351

*P*eacekeepers:
During the 1970s the
Canadian government
cultivated a reputation
of moderation and inter-
national responsibility,
symbolized by the dis-
patch of troops abroad
to maintain the peace in
international trouble spots. Sending the troops was easy:
getting them out was not. In 1965 Canadian troops were
sent to Cyprus, and stayed there for the next thirty years.
Even after they left, the island's inhabitants still had to
be separated by a garrison of UN troops. Here we see a
Canadian armoured personnel carrier deployed in Cyprus;

proved that when push came to shove, most Quebeckers drew back from supporting a romantic armed insurrection. Whatever grievances Quebeckers had, they did not persuade the overwhelming majority in that province that violence was the only or even a possible solution. With the October Crisis, terrorism came to an end in Quebec. The battle between federalism and separatism was thereafter fought in terms of electoral politics.

Photographer Frank Prazak, National Archives of Canada PA206661

October Crisis: The murdered Quebec minister Pierre Laporte was given a state funeral. Trudeau is seen outside the church.

Trudeau proved to be masterful in directing society's response to the crisis. Understanding that he was dealing in political symbols and that people required reassurance about their security, he did not hesitate to send in the army and to order the arrest of people who might have sympathized with the terrorists. Ironically, given the relatively small number of Quebec intelligentsia, many of those arrested were people he knew. Not surprisingly, most of them never forgave him — but as far as they were concerned Trudeau was already beyond the pale as a successful federalist politician.

The October Crisis did not eradicate separatism. On the contrary, it enhanced the position of the politicians who led the legal separatist movement, the Parti Québécois, founded by René Lévesque in 1968. The PQ elected the first separatist members of the Quebec legislature in the 1970 election. In the next election, 1973, it displaced the Union Nationale as the official opposition to the governing Bourassa Liberals. It became the political alternative to the Liberals, and, in an alternating political system, its ascension to power was almost guaranteed.

Photographer Jean-Marc Carisse

The problem, as far as the separatist PQ was concerned, was that the majority of Quebeckers would not vote to separate from the rest of Canada. If separatism were the issue, the Liberals would stay in power forever. Under the influence of Claude Morin, formerly a high provincial civil servant and a recent convert to separatism, the PQ undertook a two-step program. If elected, the PQ promised not to enact separatism right away, but to hold a referendum on the issue. Nor would it propose unalloyed independence, though that was what its purists favoured. It would, instead, promote "sovereignty-association," in which an independent Quebec would seek to remain economically connected to Canada. This compromise, the PQ hoped, would reassure the faint-hearted.

Opening of Parliament in 1978, showing Prime Minister Trudeau, left, and Governor General Jules Léger and Mme Léger.

The PQ had another ally in the political ineptitude of the Bourassa government. Bourassa believed that political salvation lay in achieving as much autonomy as possible within Canada. This meant reducing Ottawa's powers in the province and restricting its contact with ordinary citizens, as if the reminder that Ottawa was a real government with real powers would naturally repel the Quebec electorate. Whether or not this was true — and it was very doubtful that it was — the Bourassa government acted as if it were. It also acted to restrict the use of the English language and to promote the use of French, so as to reassure those who believed that French in Quebec was facing a constant hemorrhage in terms of daily use.

Bourassa therefore resisted Trudeau's attempts to secure a constitutional settlement. There was a near miss in a federal-provincial conference in Victoria in 1971. Trudeau had almost got all ten premiers to sign onto a package (called a "Charter") that somewhat rejigged the constitutional responsibilities of the provinces and the federal government, while providing for the amendment of the Constitution in Canada, instead of in London, as had been the practice since 1867. Bourassa appeared to agree — according to federal delegates he did agree — but, on returning to Quebec City, he found vocal disagreement among pundits and some of his advisers. The premier caved in to his critics and reneged on the Victoria Charter, and the opportunity vanished. Trudeau was unimpressed.

So, eventually, was the Quebec electorate, which drew the conclusion that Bourassa lacked both clarity and honesty. That was to some degree unfair, because Bourassa was personally not corrupt nor, on the whole, was his government. But he was unprincipled, in the sense that while promising federalism, he delivered instead a pale version of separation. This strategy won him few friends among the separatists and disappointed his federalist followers. His popularity sinking, Bourassa called a hasty election in November 1976, only to face an electorate that had decided he was not satisfactory. Instead, Quebeckers voted for the alternative party, the PQ, and René Lévesque became premier of Quebec.

The emergence of a separatist government in Quebec surprised many, including the prime minister. Trudeau immediately began an exercise in damage control. On the issue of Quebec separatism, he could still carry the majority of English Canadians with him. But disappointment with his economic record and his other policies eventually leached away his support in English Canada. The collapse of his marriage of six years with a woman thirty years his junior added to his distractions, though Canadians were impressed by the dignity with which he bore his misfortune. The government stayed in office until the last possible moment, calling an election only in May 1979.

It was an election that Trudeau narrowly lost. A minority Conservative government under Joe Clark took office at the beginning of June. Leaving Government House after submitting his government's resignation, Trudeau jumped into his Mercedes convertible and drove off. He had, after all, a life to lead.

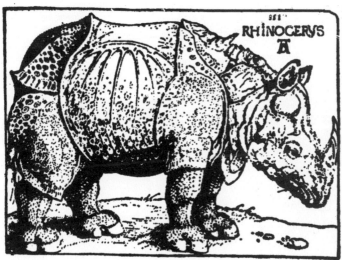

Disillusioned with the policies and corruption of old-style political parties, Montreal activists created the Rhino Party, a serio-comic movement that spread across the country in the 1970s.

Courtesy of J.L. Granatstein

CHAPTER TEN

MOVING SOUTH

National Archives of Canada C135940

*J*oe Clark's strength and weakness were that he was not Pierre Trudeau. The new prime minister was young — just forty — and had been a member of parliament for seven years. He had had no career out of politics: he had failed law school twice and completed an MA in political science, but his life was Conservative Party politics. When he won the leadership in 1976, he was so little known that the newspaper headline "Joe Who?" set the tone for his career. Strongly partisan, Clark suffered from a gangly, awkward body and his constant attempt to look serious and weighty. The only result was that he couldn't.

Clark's minority government took office and carefully planned its course, fully intending to keep its 211 campaign promises, however contradictory they might be. The Tories would govern as if they had a majority, Clark decided, thereby committing his first and fatal error. Then the government began backing away from its pledges to move the Canadian Embassy in Israel from Tel Aviv to Jerusalem, a flashpoint in world and Canadian opinion, and to sell Petro-Canada, the oil company Trudeau had created. The first issue threatened Canadian business with an Arab boycott; the second upset nationalists and Ontarians, concerned about high oil prices. Only in providing a generous welcome to thousands of Vietnamese "boat people" fleeing their repressive communist government did the Conservatives show a flash of compassion and innovation, and this initiative was largely attributable to External Affairs Minister Flora MacDonald. MacDonald did not get on well with her department's bureaucrats, but she could read the public mood. The Vietnamese were part of a new tide of refugees and immigrants from Asia, Africa, and Latin America that were beginning to pound at Canadian gates. Individual Canadians and church groups adopted thousands of these Vietnamese refugees, helping them settle in and adapt, assisted by government grants.

This outreach did little to save Clark, however. Already battered and also accused of flipflops, the new administration met Parliament — and died with its first budget. Raising gasoline taxes by 18 cents a gallon made sense in conservation terms, but not in electoral terms for a minority government. The government fell when the House managers failed to count heads, after having

Opposite: National unity was a government preoccupation as Quebec separatism strengthened. This cartoon by Rusins showed some of the symbols Canadians were supposed to cherish: the beaver, Gretzky, the Mounties, the Queen, Toronto's CN Tower, the Expos, and the Blue Jays.

passed one solitary piece of inconsequential legislation. Yet, entering another election, the Conservatives seemed eerily confident.

Obviously, Clark had banked on the Liberals appointing a new leader to fight the election. Certainly, there was consideration of this possibility in the Liberal caucus, but party insiders prevailed on Trudeau to return. Regenerated, Trudeau squashed the Tories in the election. "Welcome to the 1980s!" the once and future prime minister told the cheering Liberal crowds on election night. For his part, Clark wept in frustration and bitterness.

Trudeau's return mattered decisively in one special area. With Clark leading the nation, the Parti Québécois led in opinion polls on its coming referendum on sovereignty-association, a curious concept that called for a sovereign Quebec to form an association of equals with Canada. Whether Canada would accept such an arrangement scarcely entered the equation, but this formula, PQ strategists decided, just might persuade those afraid of sovereignty to summon up their courage and vote against Canada. After all, sovereignty-association seemed to imply that Canadian passports could be kept, along with seats in the House of Commons. Such notions were a pipe dream, a concoction of nationalism, provincialism, resentment, and wishful thinking, but many seemed to believe it.

But with Trudeau in power once more, Canada, federalism, and the status quo took the lead, regardless of René Lévesque's blandishments. Indeed, Trudeau ran the federalist campaign in Quebec brilliantly, although his cause was scarcely assisted by Claude Ryan, the former newspaper editor who had become Liberal leader. Ryan's proposals for a drastically reformed and decentralized federation were just as unpalatable as the PQ's to many in English Canada, but for now the issue was the referendum. Turning the daily direction of the campaign over to Justice Minister Jean Chrétien, who co-existed in a difficult relationship with Ryan, Trudeau intervened only three times, but with devastating effect. Lévesque had called into question Trudeau's legitimacy as a francophone because his mother was English-speaking. Trudeau seized on that racist slur to state proudly that his mother's name was Elliott and his name was Pierre Elliott. The separatists never recovered from that gaffe, and the *non* side in the May 1980 referendum won 60 percent of the

Prime Minister
Pierre Trudeau
left office in 1979
to the relief of
many Canadians.
But after the
Conservatives
stumbled into a
quick election
and party
insiders pressed
him to return,
Trudeau scored a
stunning triumph
in the election of
1980. This
proved fatal to
the separatists
in the 1980
referendum.

Photographer Jean-Marc Carisse

vote, including 52 percent of the francophone support. Teary-eyed
at the loss, Lévesque would nonetheless be re-elected in the coming
provincial election, but support for secession sank. The issue
seemed to have been put to rest, and Trudeau's vision of Canada
was supreme.

Or was it? The prime minister's main task after the 1980 victory
was to patriate the British North America Act. It was demeaning for
Canada to be obliged to secure British consent to pass constitutional
amendments simply because federal and provincial governments

The Post
Office celebrated
patriation of
the Canadian
Constitution with
a commemora-
tive stamp.

had never been able to agree on a method. Moreover, Trudeau wanted to entrench a Charter of Rights and Freedoms in the Constitution. To secure these goals, Trudeau embarked on a long and vicious round of constitutional negotiations. Eight of the provinces, including Quebec, joined a decentralist "gang" to oppose Trudeau, and only Ontario and New Brunswick stood with him. In Parliament, Clark and the Tories sniped effectively from the sidelines. Trudeau ultimately prevailed when his government decided to go it alone and to patriate the Constitution without provincial support. The British government, lobbied by provincial ministers and delegations (including expensive chefs hired to offer the best food and wine to key legislators), was not enthusiastic, but likely had no choice but to proceed.

The threat of unilateral action, together with a Supreme Court decision that equivocated on the legality of the prime minister's course, forced the provinces back to the bargaining table in November 1981. Faced with Trudeau's toughness and public impatience, the provincial front collapsed and all the provinces except Quebec signed on. Lévesque claimed he had been the victim of "a night of the long knives" when the English-speaking premiers colluded while he slept in a hotel room in Hull, but in fact he had acted in wilful blindness and had simply been outnegotiated by Trudeau and left with no support from his fellow premiers. Backed by a unanimous vote in the Quebec National Assembly, Lévesque refused to sign the Constitution, even though his province was bound by its terms, just as the others were. In 1981, with the separatist cause in ruins, that scarcely seemed to matter.

The Charter was not yet fixed in stone, however. Trudeau had been forced to give ground to the premiers, agreeing to a "notwithstanding" clause that allowed provincial governments to override the Charter with a vote of their legislatures. Moreover, the clause defining the rights of women had been watered down, and a huge and successful campaign sprang up in all provinces, including Quebec, to force the governments to accept a tough clause in this area. Trudeau had no hesitation in accepting the change, but some premiers smarted. The new Constitution Act was duly passed in the British Parliament, ending forever the appearance of colonial

Photographer Jean-Marc Carisse

subordination. Queen Elizabeth II signed the legislation on Parliament Hill in Ottawa on April 17, 1982.

Patriation of the Constitution, and particularly the inclusion of the Charter of Rights and Freedoms, was arguably the most important change in Canadians' political lives during the twentieth century. No longer was Parliament supreme. The House of Commons would propose, but the Supreme Court would ultimately decide on rights. Lawyers ruled, but pressure groups, ethnic and First Nations lobbies, and ordinary citizens had the chance to change the law. And they seized the opportunity with a will. Within a very short time Canada was well on the way to becoming as litigious as the United States, though, in that special Canadian way, the federal government funded many of those Charter challenges. The Charter of Rights and

A nattily dressed, beaming Prime Minister Trudeau with Queen Elizabeth at the Parliament Hill ceremony to mark the patriation of the Constitution in 1982.

Freedoms became an icon in the Canadian pantheon, a defining force in Canadian nationalism every bit as strong as medicare.

Trudeau's effort to protect Canadians from oil price shocks was less successful. The opening years of the 1980s saw inflation soar, and Canadians felt the pain in the grocery store and at the gas station as wages fell behind the rising cost of living. The National Energy Program of 1980, an attempt to check prices in one sector of the economy while simultaneously increasing Canadian ownership and raising federal revenues, roused passions in Alberta, making Premier Peter Lougheed and many of his citizens sound as angry with Ottawa as Lévesque and his separatists claimed to be. The federal government had moved into the oil and gas business full force, locking up land reserves, regulating prices, and imposing its will. Alberta, facing the loss of some of the revenues it had expected, reeled. The province took its lumps, suffering an economic downturn that bankrupted many, but it did not forget, and the birth of the Reform Party in 1989 was directly linked to Ottawa's refusal to countenance Alberta's claims. To Calgary oilmen, the East simply wanted to keep the West in perpetual subjugation by blocking high profits in a time of oil shortages.

The United States was just as upset with a National Energy Program that also affected American-owned oil companies. Trudeau had some sympathetic friends in the Jimmy Carter administration, but he had none in Ronald Reagan's. The movie actor president was ideologically very different from Trudeau, and Reagan's penchant for bad jokes and *Reader's Digest* trivia did not sit well with the cerebral prime minister. Relations were cool, and as Cold War tensions escalated with the Soviet Union, Trudeau's naysaying to Reagan's hardline policy won him little support for Canada's needs in Washington. At the end of 1983, in fact, Trudeau launched a "peace initiative" that took him around the world in an effort to bridge the East-West gap. In Washington, a senior administration official called the Canadian "a leftist high on pot," but Trudeau shrugged that off. When tensions began to ease between the United States and the USSR, it was not due to Trudeau's efforts, but he certainly did nothing to retard the thaw. Even so, relations between Canada and the United States were as cold as they had been since the Diefenbaker era.

All this domestic and foreign trouble played into the Progressive Conservatives' hands. Joe Clark ran an effective opposition, but his party could not forgive him for his ineptitude in losing power in 1980. His hold on power, John Fraser wrote brilliantly, "was about as secure as a first-time filleter's hold on an eel." In a 1983 party convention, Clark took two-thirds of the vote in a confidence ballot — enough to satisfy anyone but Clark. He foolishly declared that percentage as insufficient. In the leadership convention that followed, Clark lost to Brian Mulroney, a fluently bilingual oleaginous Quebecker who had never held elected office, but projected the image of a winner.

Mulroney was in his mid-forties, a poor boy from Baie-Comeau who had made his way on blarney, abundant charm, loyal friends, burning ambition, and intelligence. After losing to Clark at the leadership convention in 1976, he had bided his time, made his way upward in corporate Canada, and seized the opportunity offered him by the blown election of 1980 to displace Clark as leader. Now in charge, he won a seat in a by-election and moved into the House of Commons in late 1983. Luck was with him, for Trudeau — after a "walk in the snow" — in February 1984 announced his retirement

Trudeau's successor was John Turner, here with Liberal backroom adviser Keith Davey. Turner's time in power was very limited, as he lost the 1984 election to Brian Mulroney.

Photographer Jean-Marc Carisse

from politics. A Liberal convention chose John Turner, a former Trudeau minister with powerful corporate connections, as his successor, but as prime minister Turner's time was brief. He called an election quickly, was hammered by Mulroney in the televised leaders' debates, and lost catastrophically. Mulroney, who had promised Canadians "jobs, jobs, jobs," was in power with the largest majority in Canadian history: 211 of the 282 seats in Parliament.

Mulroney's first task was to establish "super relations" with President Reagan. The Mulroney government killed the National Energy Program and gutted the already weak Foreign Investment Review Agency — curiously without seeking anything in return from the United States. True believers, the Conservatives had declared economic nationalism dead: Canada now was "open for business." The Reaganites expressed pleasure, Mulroney was welcomed fulsomely at the White House, and the president in turn greeted Mulroney at a summit meeting in Quebec City in 1985 that featured the leaders and their spouses singing "When Irish Eyes Are Smiling" at a nationally televised gala. Unlike the prime minister, Reagan at least had the grace to look embarrassed. In return, the Americans won Canadian support in virtually every foreign policy initiative that followed. Canada, however, received very little: efforts to persuade Reagan's government to improve environmental controls in areas affecting Canada went nowhere.

Mulroney's great battle was fought for free trade with the United States. Before he came to power he had argued against reciprocity, suggesting that Canada's independence might be lost. Once in power, however, he changed his tune, and in 1985 he announced that Canada would seek to negotiate a free trade pact. The United States sensibly hung back, letting Canada be the *demandeur,* and the negotiations were long and difficult. In 1988, finally, a deal was struck that effectively eliminated tariffs, opened each country to services provided by the other, and made another National Energy Program impossible. Supporters of free trade expressed delight that the deal levelled the playing field for Canadian corporations. Critics, in contrast, believed that Canada's better social services would be lowered to the U.S. level. Proponents predicted that without an agreement, Canada would be isolated in an unpredictable world of high tariffs, so it was better to take the protection offered by the Free Trade Agreement. Others argued that tariffs, already minimal, were scarcely the issue. Rather, a psychological barrier that had made Canadians believe they were different would be breached by the agreement, never to be restored. These points were debated fiercely in meetings and at breakfast tables and, after the Liberal-dominated Senate blocked the agreement, Mulroney called an election to resolve his (the nation's) fate.

The election of 1988 was one of the most important electoral contests in Canadian history. Ordinarily, issues are not central in Canadian politics, as most voters vote their preference for leader A's or leader B's hairstyle, birthplace, religion, or mannerisms. But in 1988 the issue was crystal clear: Would Canada tie itself to the United States for good or ill or would it not? The Conservative government had the unstinting support of corporate Canada, which provided the needed money in vast amounts. The Liberals, under John Turner, who threw himself into the fight with a vigour that belied his past history of support for business, secured backing from unions and nationalist groups. After

National Archives of Canada PA196184

Turner's effective performance in a television debate with Mulroney, the Liberals sprang into the lead in the opinion polls. A brilliantly conceived Liberal advertisement showed the international border being erased by the free trade negotiators, a fair presentation of what many believed.

Prime Minister Mulroney was not widely admired by Canadians, but abroad, as at this 1987 Commonwealth Conference, he was.

Corporate advertisements soon showed the border firmly back on the map. The critics who charged that medicare was about to be sacrificed for the sake of a level playing field were countered by retired Supreme Court Justice Emmett Hall, the royal commissioner who had once pointed the way to national medicare. Finally, the desperate Progressive Conservatives launched a hard-hitting attack that reversed the tide. Mulroney was not personally popular

Integrated Ethnicity

*M*assive immigration from "non-traditional" sources began to change the face of Canadian cities. Chinese, Vietnamese, eastern Europeans, Somalis, Latin Americans poured into the country. The old Judeo-Christian religions were joined by new ones, new social attitudes, and strange new foods. Multiculturalism was government policy, and

Photographer Frank Prazak,
National Archives of Canada PA206649

although some Canadians objected, public moneys went to help new Canadians retain their identity and help ease their transition to their new homeland.

Photographer Tracy Carbert

Photographer Tracy Car

(many found his unctuousness grating and his high-spending love of power offensive) but on election night Canadians re-elected his government with a large majority, even though the anti-free trade parties had a sizable majority of the popular vote. For the first time in their history, Canadians had decisively voted against anti-Americanism and for free trade. The Free Trade Agreement was duly approved in both Parliament and the U.S. Congress, and came into force in 1989. The ink was scarcely dry before Mulroney and Reagan pressed for the inclusion of Mexico in a North American Free Trade Agreement. Immediately, corporations began moving south, taking with them the jobs Mulroney had promised to deliver. A deepening recession did not help.

The free trade battle had badly bruised everyone in Canada, especially the working class. While that fight preoccupied huge sections of the nation, the constitutional issue continued to divide Canadians yet again. When Joe Clark made overtures to the Quebec separatists, Mulroney expressed his displeasure. As party leader, however, Mulroney established links with the Quebec Liberals and the Parti Québécois, and their support helped him win his election victory in 1984. The prime minister then set out to reopen the constitutional dialogue in an attempt to bring Quebec willingly under the Constitution. At its best, Mulroney's effort was intended to bind up the wounds that Trudeau's patriation had opened. What it did, however, was revive the separatist cause, which had been thrown into the doldrums when Trudeau left office. Every time one of the premiers or newspapers expressed alarm at efforts to decentralize power to Quebec (without equivalent concessions to the other provinces) the *péquistes* took heart.

The constitutional battle was every bit as wearing as that over free trade, though tearing at the nation's fabric in different ways. The Quebec Liberals had come to power in 1985, again under Robert Bourassa, and the premier, while close to Mulroney, did not really believe that constitutional change was possible — at least not sufficiently to put Quebec's demands to rest. Nor was there much optimism in English Canada. To Mulroney's great credit, once he began he persisted in his efforts, using his considerable charm and skills at argumentation, pressing premiers and provincial opposition leaders to mobilize support. Long meetings at the government's Conference Centre in Ottawa and at the prime ministerial summer residence on Meech Lake in the Gatineau Hills finally came to fruition in 1987, creating an agreement where none had seemed possible. Quebec was declared a "distinct society," and a host of powers were to be transferred from the federal to the provincial governments. Mulroney even agreed to hand over Senate and Supreme Court nominations to the provinces, and he gave them the right to opt out of all federal programs with compensation. Moreover, there would be an annual federal-provincial meeting on the Constitution, a bargaining session to strip the remaining flesh from the carcass of Canadian federalism. To come into effect, the Meech Lake deal had to be ratified by Parliament and the provincial legislatures within three years.

Although Pierre Trudeau vigorously denounced Meech Lake as an agreement that undermined his conception of Canada, it was, in fact, to die a slow death. The Quebec "language police" or "tongue troopers" created festering resentment across the country as Bourassa enforced intolerant language laws against English speakers, English-language schools, and English-language signs in the province. Many argued that Mulroney had dealt the central government a deadly blow, and still others tied Meech and the Free Trade Agreement together, pointing to both deals as hammer blows at Canada's ability to survive. Mulroney's personal standing was low with a public that saw him as deceitful and untrustworthy, and many took the view that whatever he wanted was bound to be wrong.

The result was trouble for Meech. The three-year ratification period allowed opposition to build and it naturally produced turnovers in provincial governments. In New Brunswick and Newfoundland the Liberals took power, pledging to oppose Meech, and Premier Clyde Wells in St. John's actually meant it. There was strong opposition in Manitoba too, not least among First Nations leaders. With the clock ticking down, Mulroney called a last-ditch meeting, a chance for him (as he recklessly said in an interview) to roll the dice in a high-pressure situation. Herculean efforts almost spelled success, but, while Mulroney raged, Meech failed in June 1990 when the Newfoundland and Manitoba legislatures declined to pass the constitutional package.

Mulroney took most of the opprobrium, his tactics denounced as sleazy and deceptive. But the key result of the Meech failure was that French Quebeckers again felt humiliated and support for separatism soared. At the same time, Lucien Bouchard, a longtime Mulroney friend and his political protégé, resigned from the federal cabinet and created the Bloc Québécois to forward the separatist cause in federal politics. The fat was in the fire again.

The 1980s ended with Canada in disarray. Unemployment was high and the country in recession. Constitutional reform — whether it was needed or desired by Canadians or not — had stalled, and Quebec separatism was once again on the rise, this time with an able and charismatic leader pressing the case for it in Ottawa. What was significant, however, was that Trudeau's Constitution, Trudeau's Canada, was still intact. The Charter of Rights and Freedoms had become a part of Canadians lives, and the 1982 Constitution, however much Mulroney and the premiers wanted to change it, remained in place. The struggle was far from over, but there could be little doubt that Trudeau's vision of a bicultural federation within a multicultural framework had dominated the Canada of the 1980s, just as it had the 1970s.

INTERNATIONAL PERSONALITIES

Photographer Jean-Marc Carisse

*C*anadians began to make it on the world stage as entertainers, athletes, and personalities. Impersonator Rich Little from Ottawa became famous as a man with a thousand faces and voices, while John Candy and Dan Ackroyd changed comedy from within Second City and in television and movies.

Courtesy of Straight 'n Wicked Productions

Wayne Gretzky, gifted with extraordinary vision and superb playmaking skills, changed the way hockey was played around the world. Singer René Simard, popular in Quebec and in francophone countries, had as much impact as k.d. lang, a polished performer whose Prairie roots showed in her singing.

Photographer Jean-Marc Carisse

Photographer Jean-Marc Carisse

Photographer Jean-Marc Carisse

CHAPTER ELEVEN

THE FINAL DECADE

*T*he 1990s started well, continued badly, and ended on a note of tentative hope. Some of the events were predictable, a continuation of long-established trends in Canadian society and politics. Others were new, marking a break from tradition and the arrival of the unexpected.

Under "predictable," the events fell largely under the heading of politics. There was a crisis in Quebec-Canada relations. It had been building for thirty years, since the Quiet Revolution of the 1960s. The Meech Lake fiasco aggravated the question it was supposed to answer: What was Quebec's place in Canada? To most English Canadians the failure of Mulroney's Meech Lake strategy was well deserved: they would still have a coherent country, a nation worth belonging to. Meech was, in other words, a positive event, an affirmation of Canadian values. To most French Canadians,

Prime Minister Brian Mulroney played a very creditable role in the Commonwealth and the United Nations in pressing South Africa towards democracy. Nelson Mandela, imprisoned for years by the white regime before becoming the leader of his nation, was genuinely grateful.

Photographer Jean-Marc Carisse

225

in contrast, the rejection of Meech was a slap in the face. As a prominent Quebec economist and federalist put it some years later, when French Canada said "We love you" to English Canada, the reply was "F— off."

In Quebec, support for separatism rose. Premier Bourassa, who had fed the province's sense of grievance and resentment in the hope of forcing Meech Lake through, found that French Quebeckers now concluded they lacked respect from their English-speaking fellow citizens. Bourassa tried to divert these feelings away from immediate action. He set up study groups within the provincial Liberal Party and established a government commission to investigate matters. Fortunately he had held an election only a year before, in 1989. The Liberals had a secure majority and four more years in power. They would need them. In the meantime, Bourassa diverted the most attractive spokesman for the separatists by encouraging Lucien Bouchard, who had resigned from the Mulroney cabinet in June, to form a federal separatist party. The Bloc Québécois was duly founded out of a grab-bag of former Conservative and Liberal members of the House of Commons. For the first time, separatists had an organized party to speak for them in the federal Parliament.

The most drastic change in the new decade was the state of the economy. In the years since 1940 Canada had only rarely experienced economic ill fortune. There had been a sharp recession in 1980-81, but it was soon over. The rest of the 1980s were a time of glittering and sometimes unnerving prosperity. On the one hand, Canadians could imagine that nothing was wrong; on the other, they could prepare for the worst by buying into free trade with the United States. In 1990, however, the economy went sour. A recession gripped the country. Gross Domestic Product fell and unemployment rose, from 7.5 percent in 1989 to 11.2 percent in 1992. That decline was unfortunate, but not unique. The Europeans, France and Germany especially, had had high unemployment for years and seemed to be surviving. American unemployment rose too, as the United States entered a recession.

In the United States, concern over the economy and high unemployment helped to undermine the sitting president, George Bush, in the 1992 presidential election. And Bush had only an economic crisis to deal with. In Canada, his friend Mulroney had his hands full: a faltering economy, a constitutional crisis with Quebec, and, in the summer of 1990, a confrontation with Canada's native people. It occurred on two Indian reserves outside Montreal, Kanesatake and Kahnawake, which had been inhabited for hundreds of years by Mohawk.

The dispute began over a native cemetery that developers in Oka, Quebec, wanted to convert into a golf course. After an unsuccessful police raid, the Mohawk blockaded some of the roads that passed through their reserves. One of those roads was a main highway leading into Montreal from the south, across the Mercier Bridge. The Mohawk let it be known they were armed, as they patrolled their boundaries in camouflage uniforms and flaunted their rifles. When local and provincial police were unable to cope, the Bourassa government asked Mulroney to send in the Canadian Army, which he did. Federal troops marched into Quebec, to the relief of a French-speaking population that, in the heat of Meech Lake, was probably willing to secede from Canada. The Mohawk, English-speaking and

The confrontation at Oka pitted the army against Mohawk "warriors" in a tense confrontation that was given virtually continuous coverage on television.

Department of National Defence, ISC 90-479

with no reason to love their French-speaking neighbours, were emphatically not Quebec separatists, whatever else they may have been.

Department of National Defence, ISC 90-515

The Mohawk were well armed and supported by some American ex-soldiers. Relations between the government and the First Nations clearly had entered a new, disturbing phase.

The confrontation lasted for seventy-eight days, to the delight of the media, especially television, which seemed to have mobilized almost as many reporters and support staff as the government had troops. The troops blockaded the reserves, hoping that attrition would wear down the Mohawk, while the airwaves were full of the babble of the chattering classes. The Mohawk eventually gave up peaceably and troops occupied the reserves, arresting as many suspects as they could find.

Whatever the local causes of the Oka disturbance, a sense of grievance had been building for a long time between native and other Canadians. There was the undoubted fact that, through war, disease, numbers, and technology, immigrants from Europe (and latterly from Asia) had occupied the land that was now Canada and had driven its original inhabitants to reserves that were in most cases undesirable. Native cultures withered in the face of a society and a state that were, at best, uncomprehending. The numbers of natives declined steadily through the nineteenth century: in the 1901 census native Canadians — Indians and Inuit — numbered only 106,000,

Indians all across Canada, including these Second World War veterans wearing their Legion berets and medals, supported the Mohawk resistance at Oka.

Department of National Defence, ISC 90-761

or 1.4 percent of the total population; by 1951 they numbered 166,000, or 1.2 percent. Then things changed. The Canadian birth rate fell, but the birth rate among natives remained high, almost at Third World levels. And, in the opinion of many observers, conditions on the reserves were also Third World in nature. Poverty, alcoholism, and near universal unemployment dogged many native bands — though not all.

Politically, Indians and Inuit enjoyed a renaissance in the 1970s and 1980s, as Canadian society came to conclude that Canada's natives had been badly treated and deserved both compensation for past wrongs and protection against future depredations. In the most spectacular example, but not the only one, Indians around James Bay, dispossessed by Hydro-Québec's mega-dams in the 1960s and 1970s, exacted recognition and money from the Quebec government. The federal government officially abandoned its attempts to assimilate natives and tried, instead, to cope with the wreckage of the assimilation policy. Most prominent were the residential schools, to which

Indian children had been consigned for generations, and where they had sometimes received more abuse than education.

What the end result of this revision would be for the position of natives in Canadian society, no one could foretell. As it became clear that native status was in some ways legally advantageous — at least opening the way to the courts and to claims on the country in general — there were many new claimants. The Métis, people of mixed native-white heritage, suddenly discovered aboriginal status and a claim. The high birth rate, together with this expanded view of who was native, meant that the number of natives grew exponentially, to just over one million in 1991. Formally, however, the census counted only "status Indians," those who were entitled by treaty to claim benefits from the government: they numbered 611,000 in 1996, of whom 331,000 lived on reserves.

Throughout the 1990s the question of what would become of Canada's native peoples was much discussed, yet no clear answer could be given. Ottawa laboriously undertook to negotiate or renegotiate treaties with Indian bands. In the Arctic, the government carved out a new territory, Nunavut, by the end of the decade with a majority Inuit population and government. It also set up the Royal Commission on Aboriginal Peoples to study a broad range of issues, but after five years of analysis and many millions of dollars its report did not find success.

The commission had been appointed by the Mulroney government, but by the time it reported in 1996 there was another prime minister, another government, and another party. Mulroney left office in the summer of 1993, after achieving record unpopularity among Canadians — though less, it should be said, in Quebec than elsewhere. The recession and the constitutional failure were too much to overcome. Mulroney tried another constitutional gambit, labelled the Charlottetown Accord, only to have it shot down in a national referendum in 1992. He also shouldered the burden of an exceedingly unpopular and highly visible federal sales tax, the Goods and Services Tax, or GST. At 7 percent, it reminded Canadians of what Mulroney had done every time they approached a cash register.

A Progressive Conservative Party convention selected Kim Campbell, the defence minister, to succeed Mulroney as party leader and prime minister. Campbell had only a few months to turn things around before she was legally obliged to hold an election. It was an impossible task. When the election was called, her party's fortunes began to sink dramatically. Projections of Tory seats dropped week by week as the party leaked voters — to the Bloc Québécois in Quebec, to the Liberals in Ontario, Manitoba, and the Maritimes, and to the new Reform Party in the West. On election night a CBC satirical troupe portrayed Campbell calling for Prozac (the happy-making prescription drug of the moment) as the seat totals rolled in. Campbell lost 150 seats, including her own, and the Tory Party sank to a grand total of two in the House of Commons.

The Liberals under Jean Chrétien won 41 percent of the vote and a majority of the seats. The Liberals harvested all but one of the seats in Ontario, virtually all in Atlantic Canada, and enough sprinkled across Quebec and the West to make for a comfortable cushion in Parliament. The new leader of the opposition was Lucien Bouchard, whose Bloc Québécois won a few more seats than the Reform Party under Preston Manning. The NDP returned to Parliament, but was marginalized, cut out of Ontario and reduced to a handful of seats on the Prairies and in British Columbia.

The Chrétien government inherited a fiscal crisis that it was initially slow to grasp. The Canadian government had been dabbling in deficits for twenty years and, as the deficits accumulated, the national debt rose. So did payments on the debt. As long as the economy grew, or grew enough, the situation was bearable, though not especially desirable. When the economy shrank, as it did in 1990 and 1991, the government was forced to come to grips with a large financial problem. Mulroney had set records in raising taxes, but he set records in spending too. Canada, which once had tax rates comparable with or better than those in the United States, was now setting records for heavy taxation. The approaching election of 1993 postponed matters, but after the election the fiscal problem had to be faced.

Chrétien had little choice but to restrain federal expenditures while keeping taxes very high. The main source for savings had to be transfers of federal funds to provincial governments for such items as medicare and universities. Mulroney had already cut deeply into federal subsidies to the provinces; typically, he dipped deeper into the flow of money to Ontario, Alberta, and British Columbia than to the rest of the country, especially Quebec. As a result, there was a new harvest of grievances from those three provinces. Chrétien did not shy away from the task. He and his finance minister, Paul Martin Jr., set about to slash and burn grants for social services and education. On the expenditure side, the federal share of medicare, once 50 percent in the early 1970s, dropped to 12 or 13 percent in the late 1990s. Unemployment insurance was "reformed" so as to restrict benefits and entitlements, a process that bit especially deeply in Atlantic Canada. The deficit dropped as a result — dropped until, for the first time in a generation, the Canadian government had a surplus in 1997.

Remarkably, Chrétien and the Liberals largely escaped negative political consequences for their actions. For many years, the provinces had been taking federal money and the credit for the programs that federal money paid for. Now they had either to make up the shortfall or start paying for the programs themselves. Yet, given the taxation burden Canadians were already bearing, it was difficult to tax more. So the provinces cut their social services, including, and especially, medicare. Not surprisingly, the politicians operated on medicine with a blunt instrument. Hospitals were closed and nurses were fired. Provincial governments proclaimed they had "discovered" home care, which would take the place of hospitals, but then they failed to fund it adequately. In the heady atmosphere of Conservative (and conservative) Alberta, a Calgary public hospital was dynamited. In Quebec, which had a history of labour militancy, nurses went on strike. Despite considerable public sympathy, they lost.

The same story applied to schools, where teachers found they had to do more for less. It was a situation sometimes made worse by mistaken or short-sighted public policy, especially in Ontario, where a right-wing government marched solemnly behind its ideology into an overall reduction in public services. The right wing proclaimed an American model, where health care (private) and taxes (low) were concerned, but ignored the growth in American public spending on improving the infrastructure of American cities. But

Courtesy of the Office of the Prime Minister. Photographer Phillipe Landreville

in some areas Ottawa was little better. As a result, there was frequently a disconnection between what governments proclaimed to be the truth and what the citizenry could see around them.

A cloud of rhetoric masked these developments. No government wanted to admit the truth: that Canadians were getting poorer and could afford less. Chrétien took advantage of a United Nations survey that found Canada to be first in the world in a selected range of statistical indicators. A booster by instinct, Chrétien could hardly be blamed for using whatever good news came his way. Where good news was concerned, the 1990s were a dry season.

Canadians' personal incomes shrank in the recession of 1990-91 and did not recover lost ground until the very end of the decade. Living standards (what an individual could spend, adjusted for inflation) were 5 percent lower in 1999 than they had been in 1989. Unemployment through the decade remained high — perhaps not as high as continental Europe, but sometimes twice as high as in the United States. The evidence was all around — diminishing public services, dirtier pavements, closed shops even in the most fashionable districts, and beggars on the streets. It was a hard decade for retailers, with little or no margin for error. "Squeegee kids" (and some that were not kids) made their appearance on street corners, washing car windows whether their services were wanted or not.

The 1990s saw the disappearance of some Canadian symbols. When the century began, the Canadian Pacific Railway defined the nation. That giant corporation operated from its fortress headquarters in Montreal and from hundreds of local offices and railway yards. In the 1920s it was joined by the Canadian National Railways, and together the CP and CN left their mark on the way Canadians shipped, supped, travelled, and vacationed, as often as not in the railway hotels that stretched from Victoria to St. John's.

The latter years of the twentieth century had not been kind to the railways, which saw their business dwindle to competition from trucks and airfreight. In 1996 CP, having divested itself of its airline (CP Air, later Canadian Air) and its hotels, moved its headquarters out of Montreal to Calgary. It adopted a new corporate logo, featuring a merger of the Canadian and American flags. Canadian National changed too. It had been a government-owned company since the end of the First World War. In 1995 the government privatized CN, which moved smartly off into the private sector. The former clerk of the Privy Council, Canada's senior civil servant, took the job of president and behaved much as any other corporate executive must — in the interests of his shareholders first and foremost.

The railways were a little behind the airlines. From 1937 to 1988 the Canadian government had owned an airline, Air Canada (once called Trans-Canada Airlines, or TCA). Air Canada was privatized early on, under Mulroney. It proved an eager, indeed voracious, competitor for Canadian Airlines. In 1999 Canadian Airlines, facing bankruptcy, surrendered to Air Canada. A merger was announced and gradually implemented.

Canadian Airlines was not the only corporate casualty of 1999. Eaton's department store had been founded in the same year as Canadian Confederation. It grew along with the country through its mail-order business and, along the way, established a chain of department stores. In Toronto, where its head office and main department store were located, the company sponsored a magnificent annual Santa Claus parade each November, celebrating the advent of the year's best buying season. Television carried the spectacle across Canada and even to the United States. In the 1970s Eaton's demolished its main store and several adjacent buildings in order to build a great shopping arcade in downtown Toronto, the Eaton Centre.

Behind the glittering new store and its attached shopping palace all was not well. The catalogue business was losing money and was abandoned in 1976. The Santa Claus parade went next. It was scooped up by the city of Toronto and became a municipal artifact. Finally, in 1997, Eaton's was reorganized. The Eaton family, short of money (and, some unkindly suggested, short of talent) sold shares in the business, previously owned within the family. But injections of funds and outside management did little more than postpone disaster, which duly occurred in the summer of 1999. Eaton's went bankrupt and was sold to an American-owned rival, Sears. "Canada's department store," or what was left of it, was henceforth owned in the United States. To judge from the media, the earth had shifted. If this Canadian institution could crumble, what about the others?

There was little doubt the economy was changing. The 1988 election had been about free trade with the United States, and free trade was duly implemented the following year. It provided for an annual reduction in tariffs on Canadian-American trade, until, in 1999, they would all be gone. Trade with the United States would increase, free trade advocates promised, and it did. Exports rose by 170 percent over a decade, and imports by 150 percent. Not all of this increase resulted from free trade, though how much became something of a cottage industry for economists during the later 1990s. A reasonable guess, using the analysis of the Royal Bank of Canada, would seem to be about 25 percent of the increase in overall trade.

Free trade enthusiasts did not expect that Canadian living standards would fall during the 1990s, though, in their darker moments, opponents of free trade concluded that all kinds of negative results were likely. Analysts in the late 1990s also noted that Canadian "productivity" lagged behind American, suggesting that Canadian workers were not as efficient as American ones, or that, because of high taxes and excessive (and expensive) dependence on the state, Canadians were doomed to relative impoverishment.

Yet if we compare all the traditional areas of the economy — most manufacturing, such as automobiles, or most services or resource extraction — the "productivity gap" was not there. In fact, in many sectors of the economy, the growth in Canadian productivity exceeded that in the United States. The difference occurred in two major areas, machine tools and electronics — in short, the world of "high tech."

"High tech" is a flexible term that crowns the economy of every decade. In the 1940s and 1950s it was atomic energy, and millions of dollars of public and private investment flowed into it. In the 1960s and after it was aviation, and in the 1970s, 1980s, and 1990s it was the computer industry.

The notion that there would be a computer in every house would have astonished Canadians in the 1950s. Computers were giant sorting or counting machines, useful for mathematicians or laboratories or governments, adding, subtracting, or multiplying on a grand scale. A computer could occupy an entire building, where it would be tended by a white-coated staff, trained in the arcane engineering necessary to feed and milk the electronic beast. Like the radios of the day, computers depended on arrays of vacuum tubes and miles of wiring to function. Acolytes spent years learning the computer programming that allowed them to "talk" to the computer via cards with holes punched in them. IBM, a business machine manufacturer, placed a computer on display at its New York headquarters in 1952.

The invention of transistors, using silicon, and integrated circuits (chips) in the 1950s shrank computers, first to the size of a room and then, in the late 1970s, to desk size. (Transistor radios were a byproduct of these developments, and appeared in Canada in the late 1950s.) The computers of the 1960s and 1970s were still very expensive, renting in Canada from $135,000 a month to a bar-

National Archives of Canada PA206643

gain $350. Companies that could afford them bought their own, and, by the early 1960s, twenty-four Canadian universities owned computers. IBM opened offices across Canada to manage this new and growing market.

Photographer Tracy Carber

It was the marriage of the computer with the typewriter that offered the first breakthrough into the mass consumer marketplace. By the early 1970s electric typewriters, the office miracle of the 1940s, had gone about as far as they could. Now, computer "hardware" (the machines) and "software" (programs) were adapted to typewriter use and sold to offices. Starting around 1970, that was where most Canadians first saw them. IBM, which had dominated the electric typewriter market, developed a personal computer, or PC, which could be operated without expensive training. Like early televisions, PCs, when they first became widely available in the mid-1980s, were sold at a price ($2,300-$9,000) only the affluent could afford. Unlike televisions, they rapidly improved in quality and capacity as they dropped in price. The development of computers with greater and greater capacity spawned a "software" industry with programs designed so that any idiot could learn how to run them. The dominant operating system, though not the easiest or probably the best, came from Microsoft via IBM. The rival Apple brand proved unable to match IBM's massive investment and marketing system. Prices declined through the 1990s while capacity and quality improved, making the computers of 1999 far more powerful than their predecessors at the beginning of the decade.

The Canadian census started to count computers. In 1994, 6.2 million Canadians used computers on the job. Secretarial jobs were redefined and stenographic ones — dictation and typing — had, by the end of the century, almost vanished. In 1997, 36 percent of Canadian households (4.2 million) owned computers, with the highest proportion in the three most prosperous provinces of British Columbia, Alberta, and Ontario. It would be only a matter of time before the others caught up, as computer ownership moved towards near universality.

At first, computers were imported from the United States, and "Silicon Valley," outside San Francisco, was the acknowledged centre of the industry. Canadian companies were not far behind, however. Mitel in Ottawa spawned a host of imitators and descendants, creating Canada's own version of Silicon Valley in the capital's western suburbs.

With computers, by the 1990s, came the Internet and e-mail. E-mail was already common inside companies by the mid-1980s, but took longer to spread to households. The Internet had actually begun in the late 1950s as an American defence project. By 1983 it had developed to the point that a formal agreement and system, called the Internet, was established. The World Wide Web (www) came later, in 1989, the product of a European laboratory. Letters, announcements, research, and sales (e-commerce) followed. The form and possibly the nature of communication were changing. Books and the printed word generally had a physical form and had to be transported. Like chairs or caviar, they could be counted and taxed — and restricted or confiscated. They were, in other words, subject to national regulation and even management. Radio and television had a restricted range until the 1970s, when satellite technology made it possible to leapfrog national barriers and physical distance. Still, the equipment was expensive and the temptation marginal, and regulators made a nuisance of themselves with threats of confiscation or other forms of punishment.

The Internet travelled, by the late 1990s, either on telephone wires or on cable networks into offices and households. Access to the Internet was ubiquitous: other forms of communication even acknowledged the fact, as television networks and radio stations developed their own Web sites and invited their audience to "tune in" via the Internet. Technology made it possible to "download" music, books, and art to the computer at home. What this capability would mean for copyright nobody knew; what it meant for "broadcast regulation" was only too apparent. The Internet jumped frontiers, and the authorities scrambled to catch up.

The convenience of computers and the Internet was undeniable. Computer shopping, computer banking, and computer office management streamlined a range of functions and changed the shape of the workplace — and with it, Canadians' daily life. Take the case of banks and banking. In the early 1970s a bank was, in appearance, similar to what it had been for a hundred years: tellers behind a counter dispensing money and recording transactions, and crocodiles of customers in front. Banks kept restricted hours — 10 a.m. to 3 p.m. four days a week, with an extension to 6 p.m. on Fridays. Cash was something available only from tellers in banks, and woe betide the unfortunate caught short on a weekend. Credit cards

Photographer Tracy Carbert

Amazingly, bank machines put cash into people's hands twenty-four hours a day. It was a revolution.

crept into daily life in the 1960s and, by the mid-1970s, were virtually universal. Banks began to stretch their hours. Bankers early saw the advantage of machines that could count and sort, and, behind the scenes, computers were being installed. The first outward sign was the arrival of automated teller machines (ATMs) in the early 1970s, mirrored on the other side by the disappearance of tellers and the closure of branches. Some banking services were available from machines, and the banks employed growing numbers of computer technicians.

Canadian habits were changing in other ways too. From the First World War until the 1960s, official puritanism kept a firm grip on society. Liquor was hard to get, drugs were the province of small numbers of the depraved, and gambling was a hushed secret. Lotteries were restricted to the annual Irish Hospitals Sweepstakes — a good cause, if an illegal one, for sweepstakes were prohibited by Canadian law. Things changed, and by the 1990s Canada became fertile ground not only for lotteries but also for gambling. Governments, starved for revenue to pay for their services or to offset their abundant debts, knew that the "tax on stupidity" was readily available — the desire to get something for nothing. Provincial governments and Indian bands alike lunged at these sure-fire profits. By 1995 gambling accounted for $4.6 billion in Canada; in Ontario, for $1.5 billion of provincial revenue. In the later 1990s gambling, including casinos and slot-machine dens, was a major growth industry in Canada. The government's liquor monopoly earned a profit of $650 million in 1996-97. That same year, 72 percent of Ontarians over the age of twelve drank, slightly less than the Canadian average. The group with the highest propensity to drink was Newfoundland males between twenty and forty-four (92.5 percent), closely followed by the same age cohort from Manitoba (90.5 percent).

Government did not pose a universal threat to the health and solvency of its citizens, however. In one area in particular government action had stimulated a change in lifestyle that would instantly have been noticed by a visitor to the 1990s from the 1950s: smell. At mid-century the scent of tobacco was everywhere and, smokers or not, people carried the odour with them. Homes and offices reeked with smokes that ranged from fragrant to acrid, and no room was complete without a set of ashtrays, often overflowing with butts and ash. On stage and in movies, sophisticated characters dangled and dawdled with cigarettes, role models to be imitated by people of both sexes and all ages.

Starting in the 1960s, health warnings began to be heard, first in the United States, but soon in Canada too. Smoking might cause disease — especially cancer of the lungs or the lips, or it might start off a severe case of emphysema. Smoking began to decline, to the distress of Canada's cigarette companies and tobacco farmers. In the 1970s the tobacco farmers of southern Ontario began to convert to peanuts; tobacco smokehouses became a curiosity whose purpose only the older generation could divine. Cigarette smoking declined, though it did not disappear altogether. Governments denounced the habit, but could not bring themselves to do without the tax revenue that the "sin" of smoking produced. In any case, the futile prohibition of alcohol in the 1920s left a lasting impression on lawmakers. Banning sin was not likely to work; taxing it worked much better. After thirty years of pressure and propaganda, much of it direct from government, only 23.6 percent of Canadians smoked in the 1990s. (The heaviest smokers, relative to the rest of the population, were in Quebec — both sexes — and among males in the Maritime provinces.) If people smoked, it was usually no longer indoors, where it was banned from offices and other public spaces. Small groups of puffers congregated miserably outside in all kinds of weather, and the entrances to major buildings were marked by a trail of butts.

As a public health measure, the anti-smoking campaign was reasonably successful. And so, in the 1990s, it was not Canadians but their country that had a near-death experience. The collapse of Meech Lake and the failure of the Mulroney government's constitutional program awakened French Quebeckers' dormant addiction to separatism. Under the federalist government of Premier Bourassa, the francophone population had hoped to make some gains from the profitable autonomy he promised. Instead, they found they had

Photographer Tracy Carbert

stimulated an almost forgotten craving for separatism. Bourassa's successor, Daniel Johnson, was the brother of one Quebec premier and the son of another (each in a different party). This Johnson, a federalist, joined the Quebec Liberals, who held that Quebec could achieve nearly complete autonomy within Canada while still enjoying the security and economic benefits of Canadians. The Liberals did not acknowledge that Quebeckers had common interests with other Canadians and in large measure shared a similar lifestyle, so the pursuit of autonomy was pointless, if not counterproductive. Such an argument might have offended "moderate" nationalists.

Johnson and the Liberals were nudged out of office in a provincial election in the fall of 1994. The separatist Parti Québécois under

Concern for health — and rising cancer rates— led governments to limit places where smokers could indulge.

Jacques Parizeau took office with a clear majority of seats, though not a majority of the popular vote. Parizeau, a veteran of twenty-five years of separatist politics, was a firm believer in his cause. He despised the half-hearted strategy that had made earlier separatist leaders combine their vision of separatism with a promise of security through "association" with Canada. But the problem remained: such a platform might not win in an election. Quebeckers, pollsters reported, were nervous about the outcome from an independence vote pure and simple. And so "moderate" separatists, led by Lucien Bouchard, the leader of the Bloc Québécois in Ottawa, imposed a compromise on Parizeau, forcing him to promise once again that Quebec would seek association with Canada after it had voted in a referendum to separate from Canada.

Parizeau agreed, perhaps believing that the vote was the thing, the important psychological barrier, and that afterwards it would be swiftly apparent that English Canada would not agree to a deal on any terms that separatist Quebeckers would accept. Parizeau then called a referendum for October 30, 1995, and launched his campaign in a solemn ceremony in a Quebec City theatre. Behind the scenes, he prepared for a unilateral declaration of independence, one that was not conditional in any way on a negotiated association with the rest of Canada. But Parizeau's campaign stumbled: he failed to inspire the majority of Quebeckers, and his promises did not command confidence. The federalist forces, divided between the national government in Ottawa under Jean Chrétien and the opposition in Quebec City led by Johnson, confidently believed they would not only prevail but would win by 60 percent or better. At mid-campaign, Parizeau, scenting defeat, turned the battle over to Bouchard.

The electorate was already beginning to rethink its early federalist inclination and the separatist camp picked up steam. Independence would transform Quebec, Bouchard promised, like a "magic wand." Waving the wand, he inspired separatists and depressed federalists. Chrétien panicked: at the last moment he issued a spate of promises designed to encourage the belief that Quebec really could win more autonomy, just as the Quebec Liberals wanted. A huge federalist rally, organized by Brian Tobin, Chrétien's minister of fisheries, and attracting Canadians from across the country, took place in Montreal at the end of the campaign.

On referendum day separatist militants took steps to slow or negate the vote in areas likely to support the status quo. Parizeau, now confident of victory again, prepared a package of emergency measures to shore up the Canadian dollar, which he knew would come under immediate downward pressure once the vote for independence was in. The vote took a few hours to tally, but by 9 p.m.

The 1995 Quebec referendum was won by Canada with the narrowest of margins. The question had been confusing, but if Bouchard had won, the consequences could have been very serious.

the result was clear: separatism had almost won, but not quite. The federalists had squeaked out a win, 50.6 to 49.4 percent. Parizeau, deeply disappointed, made an incautious speech blaming "money" and "ethnics" for the loss. Probably "money," not wanting to lose its value, and "ethnics," not wanting to lose their country, did swing the result, for the majority of French-speaking Quebeckers voted for independence, conditional or not. The referendum seemed to promise trouble for the future, for with success so close, would the separatists not try again, and soon?

They did not. The 1995 referendum was exhausting. Life went on, other problems appeared, and elections came and went. Bouchard, now premier, sent off occasional fulminations from Quebec City, and Chrétien replied from Ottawa. Most Quebeckers, it appeared, thought another referendum would not change anything, and by 1999 many were giving clear signs that enough was, finally, enough. Would the "many" become "most"? That question remained unanswered as Canada's century drew to a close.

CHAPTER TWELVE

CONCLUSION

National Archives of Canada C132141

espite media concerns about high taxes, a brain drain of skilled and high-tech workers, and ongoing worries about the future of Quebec in Canada, the nation that entered the twenty-first century seems poised to soar. The harsh deficit fighting that marked the 1990s has moderated as budget surpluses have returned. The economy is booming and unemployment is relatively low, along with inflation. For a change, Quebec separatism is in the doldrums, if only because battle fatigue has gripped everyone in Quebec and Canada. We think we know why. We believe that the story we have told in this book explains why Canada has been and will continue to be a success.

In essence, Canada is a great bus lumbering down the road. There is room for everyone, including the Québécois, so long as they accept that the bus, while it may make stops and follow occasional detours, is heading in a definite direction. That direction is not, as some have suggested, towards Canada's becoming the first post-modern nation, an illusionary state, a minimalist holding operation in which racial, regional, and other sub-national forces go their own way. Nor is it towards world power, mesianism, or a pan-Canadian nationalism. Instead, the bus is going down the middle of the road because drivers and passengers alike understand that they must cooperate to thrive in an inhospitable climate and must work together or slide into the American maw.

Opposite: Opportunity and the chance for a new start. That was what Canada has always offered immigrants from all over the globe.

Parti Québécois Premier René Lévesque tried and failed to win his 1980 referendum, despite trimming his policies to suit the electorate. This cartoon captured the differences between radical separatism and Lévesque's moderation.

National Archives of Canada C147378

"ONE CRISIS AT A TIME, DAMMIT!"

We forget that many things unite all those riders on the Canadian bus. A shared history is one, though, regrettably, history is scarcely taught in our schools any longer. Where it is, the past is filtered through the very fine mesh created by the education ministries of ten provinces. The result, when combined with the prevailing political correctness that stifles debate, is schools that teach victimology, regionalism, and provincialism; unfortunately, they almost never teach the nation's history. History can divide, of course, and, as we have seen, Canadian history, like that of virtually every

National Archives of Canada C147377

Above: Canadians frequently groaned about their lot, with nascent western separatism, high taxes, inflation, and controls all dominating the political stage at different points. Grumbling seemed to be the Canadian condition.

nation, represents no triumph of the brotherhood of man. But a nation, by one definition, is a group of a people who have done great things in the past and will do so again. The past is important, in other words, as much as the present and future. Québécois know this and proclaim this understanding on their licence plates; Canadians, the most ahistorical people on earth, do not.

Despite the efforts of those who have trashed and distorted it, history still has the power to unite us. Ours is the history of extraordinarily diverse peoples who have built a nation that is admired for its tolerance and envied for its wealth. It is the history of a people who have struggled to stay separate from, yet closely aligned with, the United States. It is the story of an unmilitary nation that has never fought a war of aggression, but whose servicemen and women have demonstrated courage in battle and skill in peacekeeping. It is the history of a people who blush and stammer at their virtues and become inflamed with pride only at their hockey victories. It is the history of a people who are very nationalistic while eschewing the excesses of nationalism.

The future lay with the nation's children. Mass education tried to prepare them for life in a world of globalization; whether they would understand what it meant and means to be Canadian was very much in question.

Photographer Tracy Carber

251

The twentieth century belongs to Canada, Laurier said. He was right to predict a great future for his nation, but Canada will require leadership skills equal to his if the nation is to thrive and prosper in the new millennium.

National Archives of Canada C15568

The Canadian story is that of the bicultural Canada that exists within the multicultural state. It is the tension and, yes, affection that indissolubly links Quebec and Canada. This bicultural/multicultural Canada is distinct, different enough from the United States that it can remain integrated with it, yet still independent. The tragedy of Quebec separatism is that, if it succeeds, it may well destroy the basis of Canadian—and Québécois—independence. Without the biculturalism that Quebec provides, there is little to differentiate Canada from the United States. Without Canada as its interlocutor within North America, an independent Quebec, if it hopes to trade and operate in the continental economy, would be obliged to become more open to the English language than it is now. Quebec's only other option is to become a francophone theme park for tourists from the United States, a Louisiana with poutine and without Zydeco. That is no fate for a proud people who have built Canada.

Wilfrid Laurier was the model Canadian for all times. He knew in 1904 that his country had a great future, and he was right in his judgments: the twentieth century really would belong to Canada and Canadians. With political skill and courage, with calmness and civility, Canada, with Quebec a willing partner, will remain free, united, and prosperous. Then the twenty-first century, like its predecessor, will be ours as well.

FURTHER READINGS

There are literally thousands of books on twentieth-century Canada, far too many to list, let alone read. There are memoirs and biographies, academic histories and popular accounts, social scientists' ruminations and literary studies. What we have tried to provide here is a brief listing of some readily available books.

The authors of this book have both written texts that are good places to begin. Robert Bothwell, John English, and Ian Drummond, *Canada since 1900* (Toronto 1987) and *Canada since 1945* (Toronto 1989) offer detailed, thorough, often humorous accounts. J.L. Granatstein et al., *Nation: Canada since Confederation* (Toronto 1990) is a hefty tome that combines a political narrative with the social history of the country.

The volumes in the Canadian Centenary Series that cover the twentieth century do so with some thoroughness down to 1967: R. Craig Brown and R. Cook, *Canada, 1896-1921* (Toronto 1974), J. Thompson and A. Seager, *Canada, 1922-1939* (Toronto 1985), Donald Creighton, *Canada, 1939-1957* (Toronto 1976), and J.L. Granatstein, *Canada, 1957-1967* (Toronto 1986). Creighton may have been the country's greatest historian, but this volume is far from his best work.

There are relatively few economic histories. By far the best is K. Norrie and D. Owram, *A History of the Canadian Economy* (Toronto 1991). Michael Bliss' *Northern Enterprise* (Toronto 1987) is the finest study of Canadian business.

For histories of aboriginal peoples in this century, the foremost volume is J.R. Miller, *Skyscrapers Hide the Heavens*, 3rd ed. (Toronto 2000). Miller's *Shingwauk's Vision* (Toronto 1996) gives a fair account of the depressing story of native residential schools.

The twentieth century was a time of war and cold war, and there are many studies of these themes. The official histories make a fine start. On the Great War, see G.W.L. Nicholson, *The Canadian Expeditionary Force, 1914-1919* (Ottawa 1955) and *The Canadians in Italy* (Ottawa 1957), C.P. Stacey, *The Victory Campaign* (Ottawa 1960), and Stacey's magisterial account of wartime policy, *Arms, Men and Governments* (Ottawa 1970). There are three volumes of *The Official History of the Royal Canadian Air Force* (Toronto 1980-94). The official naval history is yet to be published, but Marc Milner's *Canada's Navy* is very good. On the Korean War, see D.J. Bercuson, *Blood on the Hills* (Toronto 1999). Other books that cover wartime Canada in a readable way include R. Bothwell and W. Kilbourn, *C.D. Howe* (Toronto 1979), J.L. Granatstein, *Canada's War* (Toronto 1974), James Eayrs' multi-volume *In Defence of Canada* (Toronto 1960-83), Chubby Power's memoir *A Party Politician* (Toronto 1966), and Paul Martin (the father), *A Very Public Life*, 2 vols. (Ottawa 1983-85).

There is one excellent study of the Liberal Party — Reg Whitaker's *The Government Party* (Toronto 1977) — and one very good journalistic account, Christina McCall Newman, *Grits* (Toronto 1982). Sir Wilfrid Laurier, William Lyon Mackenzie King, Louis St. Laurent, Lester Pearson, Pierre Elliott Trudeau, and Jean Chrétien all have had biographies. King left a superb diary (the four volumes of *The Mackenzie King Record* [Toronto 1960-70]), Pearson wrote a splendid three-volume memoir, but Trudeau's ghost-written memoir is dreadful. The best prime ministerial biography, John English's *Life of Lester Pearson*, 2 vols. (Toronto 1989-92), is excellent. On the Conservatives, see John English, *The Decline of Politics* (Toronto 1977) and J.L. Granatstein, *The Politics of Survival* (Toronto 1967), which treat what was, until the 1990s, the Tories' low point. There are also readily available biographies of Robert Borden, Arthur Meighen, R.B. Bennett, John Diefenbaker, and Brian Mulroney, the finest of which is Denis Smith, *Rogue Tory* (Toronto 1995) on Diefenbaker. The CCF is best approached through Leo Zakuta, *A Protest Movement Becalmed* (Toronto 1964) and Walter Young, *The Anatomy of a Party* (Toronto 1969). The University of Toronto Press has published a long run of historical and socio-logical books on the Social Credit movement. The Reform Party is too new for serious study, the Canadian Alliance even more so. One good book is Trevor Harrison, *The Passionate Intensity* (Toronto 1995).

There are fine histories of virtually all the provinces, with Quebec the best served — in quantity — and Ontario the least. Perhaps Ontario really does think of itself as the nation. Robert Bothwell's *Short History of Ontario* (Edmonton 1986) provides what its title promises. For Quebec, Robert Rumilly's *Histoire de la Province de Québec*, 41 vols. (Montreal 1940-69) is interesting but not always reliable. More practical is P.A. Linteau et al., *L'Histoire de la Québec contemporain*, 2 vols. (Montréal 1979-86). On the West, see Gerald Friesen, *The Canadian Prairies* (Toronto 1984), particularly for the years before 1941, and on the East the best source is *Atlantic Canada after Confederation*, the second volume of P. Buckner and D. Frank, eds., *The Acadiensis Reader* (Fredericton 1985). There are also sound biographies of several premiers, notably Maurice Duplessis, Joey Smallwood, Mitch Hepburn, and Leslie Frost.

For social history, a good beginning is John Porter's classic *Vertical Mosaic* (Toronto 1965). Neil Sutherland's *Growing Up* (Toronto 1997) looks at child-hood through most of the century, while Doug Owram's *Born at the Right Time* (Toronto 1996) splendidly studies the baby boom generation. Given the cen-trality of public opinion polling for the last two-thirds of the century, it is surprising that Daniel Robinson's *Measure of Democracy* (Toronto 1999) is the sole first-rate history of this theme. On women, see A. Prentice et al., *Canadian Women: A History* (Toronto 1988), and J. Parr and M. Rosenfeld, *Gender and History in Canada* (Toronto 1996).

INDEX

Foreign Investment Review Agency, 191, 214
Foster, Sir George, 28
Ferdinand, Archduke Franz, 51
Fraser, Blair, 150
Fraser, John, 174, 213
Frontier College, 95

G

General Agreement on Tariffs and Trade (GATT), 150
George VI, King, 107
Ginger Group, 78
Goods and Service Tax (GST), 230
Gordon, Walter, 171, 179
Gould, Glenn, 180
Gray, James, 92-93, 94
Green, Howard, 169
Gretzky, Wayne, 221
Groulx, Lionel, 8, 118

H

Halifax, 3, 9-10, 32, 54, 61-62, 93, 96, 143
Hall, Emmett, 215
Hamilton, 12, 43, 143
Harkness, Douglas, 168-170
Hawkins, "Rompin'" Ronnie, 189
Hepburn, Mitch, 94, 100, 113
Hitler, Adolf, 104, 106, 111, 115, 125, 131
Holt, Sir Herbert, 10
Houde, Camillien, 112-113
Howe, Clarence D., 119, 141, 156-157
Hudson Bay, 14
Hudson's Bay Company, 13-14, 96
Hughes, Sir Sam, 53-55
Hull, 13, 210

I

Iron Ore Company of Canada, 150

J

Johnson, Daniel (Liberal), 242-243
Johnson, Daniel (Union National), 181

K

Kennedy, John F., 168, 169-170
King, William Lyon Mackenzie, 76, 78-80, 83, 91, 101-103, 104-106, 111-116, 118, 126-127, 130, 132, 154, 173, 186
Komagata Maru, 33-34, 35-36
Korean War, 152-156

L

Lakehead University, 178
lang, k.d., 221
LaPalme, Robert, 102
Lapointe, Ernest, 112, 115
Laporte, Pierre, 197-198, 200
Laurendeau, André, 118
Laurier, Sir Wilfrid, ix, x, 6-8, 36, 51-52, 54, 58-59, 76, 252-253
Laval University, 178
Leacock, Stephen, 10, 27
League of Nations, 78, 154
Leduc, 149-150
Lesage, Jean, 171
Lethbridge, 38
Lethbridge University, 178
Lévesque, Réne, 171, 185, 200, 202, 208-209, 210
Lightfoot, Gordon, 189
Little, Rich, 220
Lloyd George, David, 58, 60
London (Ontario), 93
Lougheed, Peter, 212

M

MacArthur, General Douglas, 153
MacDonald, Flora, 207
Macphail, Agnes, 86-87
Manning, Preston, 231
Marchand, Jean, 134
Marshall, George C., 131
Martin, Paul, 181
Martin Jr., Paul, 232
McClung, Nellie, 86
McEwen, Marshal "Black Mike," 123
McGeer, Gerry, 96
McGill University, 7, 10, 178
McLuhan, Marshall, 190
McNaughton, General Andrew, 126

Sifton, Clifford, 36-38, 43, 46
Simard, René, 221
Simon Fraser University, 178
Somme, Battle of, 56
Sparling, J. W., 27
St. John's, 146
St. Laurent, Louis, 132, 135, 146, 160
St. Lawrence Seaway and Power
    Project, 151-152, 156, 165-166
Stalin, Joseph, 111, 152
Stanfield, Robert, 181
Statute of Westminster, 79, 111
Sudbury, 143, 157
Suez Crisis, 159-160

T

Tobin, Brian, 243
Toronto, xii, 10, 12, 22, 29, 31, 54, 84, 96,
    100, 124, 142-143, 147, 154, 156, 165,
    166, 175, 177, 189, 191, 194-195, 235
Toronto Maple Leafs, 143
Treaty of Versailles, 68
Trudeau, Charlie, 85
Trudeau, Pierre Elliott, 118, 134, 181,
    185-187, 191-193, 197-199, 200-203,
    208-213, 218-219
Truman, Harry, 151, 153-154
Turner, John, 214, 215

U

United Nations, 131, 154
Université de Québec à Montréal
    (UQAM), 178
University of Alberta, 178
University of British Columbia, 178
University of Manitoba, 178
University of Regina, 178
University of Saskatchewan, 178
University of Toronto, 22, 178

V

Van Horne, Sir William, 10, 43
Vancouver, xii, 29, 32, 35, 45, 64, 84, 96,
    147, 175, 177
Victoria, 6, 147, 202
Victoria, Queen 4-6, 8, 13

Vietnam War, 177-178, 188
Vimy Ridge, 57

W

War Measures Act, 54, 197-198
Wells, Clyde, 218
Western University, 178
Wilson, Woodrow, 66
Windsor, 124, 189
Winnipeg, 3, 13, 18, 29, 31, 43, 84, 99,
    157
Winnipeg General Strike, 68, 76
Winters, Robert, 181
Women's Royal Canadian Navy
    (WRCN), 117
Woodsworth, Reverend J.S., 30
World Grain Exhibition, 97

Y

York University, 178
Young, Neil, 189

Z

Zedong, Mao, 152

ACKNOWLEDGEMENTS

We have, as always, benefited from the assistance of others. Bill Kaplan, Canada's title-*meister,* made up our minds on what to call this book. Gabrielle Nishiguchi did a splendid, imaginative job of finding photographs and illustrations. Michael Callaghan laid out the book and provided additional images on short notice. Rosemary Shipton, our long-time editor both individually and collectively, yet again worked her miracles. We have also been helped greatly by researchers Serge Vucetic, Mike Morgan, and especially Gail Corbett. Our gratitude to them all.

RB and JLG
Toronto and Port Hope
July 2000

*This book was set using
Galliard, Palatino, and Utopia fonts*